ADVANCE PRAISE

"Lana Melman shines a light on how antisemitism impacts the entertainment industry and on the hypocrisy that underpins the BDS movement."
—BEN SILVERMAN, EMMY AND GOLDEN GLOBE AWARD–WINNING PRODUCER BEHIND *THE OFFICE, JANE THE VIRGIN,* AND *UGLY BETTY,* AMONG MANY OTHERS

"An eye-opening, justifiably angry book set in the high-octane world of entertainment, where artists have become fearful that their livelihoods will be ended and reputations ruined with a tweet. A must-read by industry insider, Lana Melman, for anyone interested in the arts, artists, Hollywood and the real threat of antisemitism to our industry."
—DAVID ZUCKER, WRITER/DIRECTOR/PRODUCER (*THE NAKED GUN* FRANCHISE, *SCARY MOVIE 3, SCARY MOVIE 4, SCARY MOVIE 5,* AND *AIRPLANE!*)

"Lana Melman's truth-telling is refreshing, accurate, and powerful. If this book does not wake up the woke and the rest of us to the dangers of cancel culture and Jew-hatred, I don't know what will."
—RABBI STEVE LEDER, AUTHOR OF *THE BEAUTY OF WHAT REMAINS*

"*The relentless attack on Israel, the Jewish state, through BDS is carefully delineated in Lana Melman's new book. It is an unvarnished indictment of those antisemitic forces in the arts who seek to stifle other artists to suit their political agendas.*"

—RABBI DAVID BARON, TEMPLE OF THE ARTS

"*I would like to thank Lana Melman and Liberate Art for everything you do to counter the attempt of a cultural boycott against Israel.*"

—SAM GRUNDWERG, FORMER CONSUL GENERAL OF ISRAEL IN LOS ANGELES

ARTISTS UNDER FIRE

The BDS War Against
Celebrities, Jews, and Israel

Sue,
I hope this book
inspires you to action.
Lana Melman

LANA MELMAN

LIONCREST
PUBLISHING

ARTISTS UNDER FIRE
The BDS War against Celebrities, Jews, and Israel

FIRST EDITION

ISBN   978-1-5445-2850-2 *Hardcover*
        978-1-5445-2848-9 *Paperback*
        978-1-5445-2849-6 *Ebook*

I dedicate this book to the people I have loved and lost

and to my children and their children, to ensure they will always

have a place to go, no matter how the winds blow.

CONTENTS

DISCLAIMER

When I refer to the Boycott, Divestment, and Sanctions (BDS) campaign, I am speaking about the overall movement and not any identifiable group, person, or entity. Throughout this book, I group individuals into different categories, such as "Zealots," "Israel Bashers," or "Fellow Travelers," depending on how I view their support or lack of support for the BDS campaign and based on their public statements and actions regarding Israel. Some artists and others quoted in this book have subsequently retracted or apologized for their antisemitic or anti-Israel comments. I have not noted those later statements in all cases because it is my belief that after-the-fact apologies and retractions do little to reverse the damage done by their initial remarks. While some may disagree with my characterizations, they are my opinions based on my observations, research, interviews with others, and years of work in the field.

Third-party quotes have been largely unedited to preserve their authenticity.

INTRODUCTION

I was introduced to Jew-hatred many years ago. My mother taught me about the Holocaust when I was just nine years old. My grandmother whispered terrifying stories about pogroms in her native Russia. My dad talked of growing up in Los Angeles, where the signs in shops and restaurants said, "No Negroes… No Jews…No dogs allowed."

The parents of a grammar school friend were both survivors who met after the camps. Crude ink numbers peeked out from under my friend's mother's cotton sleeve as she made us sandwiches for lunch. Her dad's tattoo was visible on hot summer days when he puttered around the house in a T-shirt and shorts.

My parents explained to me that we Jews had to live in our own neighborhoods, go to our own schools, and join our own clubs because we were not allowed in the non-Jewish neighborhoods, non-Jewish schools, and non-Jewish clubs.

My parents were willing to accept the discrimination they faced in American society. They did not go where they were not allowed. They were of the same generation as the Holocaust survivors, who were part of their community and who wore the scars of Jew-hatred tattooed on their forearms. My dad fought in the war, and the murder of European Jewry was personal to him. Millions of Jews—men, women, and children; fathers, mothers, sons, and daughters—perished in the ovens and killing fields of Europe during the Second World War, victims of the Nazi regime and the indifference of their neighbors.

While I was raising my children and working in Hollywood as an entertainment attorney and then creative executive-turned-writer/producer, I wanted to believe that the dark cloud of antisemitism had finally passed over us. After all, doors that were shut to our parents were open to us. Israel was hailed as a miracle by Jews and admired by all.

I was wrong.

I was unaware that strains of antisemitism were creeping back into universities in the West in the form of antizionism. I did not know that a coalition of individuals and organizations called the Boycott, Divestment, and Sanctions (BDS) campaign would seek to isolate Israel—the only true haven for millions of Jews across the globe—economically, academically, and culturally as a path to its ultimate dissolution. I never imagined that this politically motivated campaign would use the celebrity of artists to spread destructive lies about the Jewish homeland and poison hearts and minds across the world.

Today, Jews are being attacked on the streets in New York, Los Angeles, and Toronto. In London, cars drive through Jewish neighborhoods as their passengers scream out calls for violence against us.

On the right, it is the self-proclaimed neo-Nazis who murder Jews in synagogues and grocery stores. In the United States alone, we have far-right antisemitic organizations such as the Ku Klux Klan, the White Aryan Resistance, and the Proud Boys. Clothing bearing the emblem "Camp Auschwitz" or emblazoned with the letters and numbers "6MWE"—a neo-Nazi code for "six million murdered during the Holocaust were not enough"—has shown up at political rallies and is sold online.

Jew-hatred, however, holds no allegiance to politics. It was rampant under the czars in pre-revolutionary Russia, infected the Communist Party in the Soviet Union, and is intrinsic to Islamic extremism, whose followers chant, "Death to Israel" in the streets of Iran.

Almost all Jews recognize Jew-hatred when it comes from the far-right and Islamism. Most American Jews are Democrats, and it is easy to call out Jew-hatred when you see it on the other side of the political spectrum. We are all brave enough to do that. The BDS campaign against Israel and the antisemitism it is fomenting, however, is coming from the left. And often, not just the far left.

As a third-generation Democrat whose liberalism had been a cornerstone of her political life, it was difficult for me to believe that members from the "same side of the aisle" as me were guilty of a Jew-hatred that disguised itself as virtue. Ten years of work combating the cultural arm of the BDS campaign (hereinafter referred to as the "cultural boycott campaign") have sadly taught me that it is true. Antisemitism is not blue or red; it is color blind.

Some people are quick to rationalize the antisemitic undercurrent in BDS messaging by pointing to one or another Israeli policy they do not agree with while ignoring the many other policies they do agree with, such as freedom of speech and women and LGBTQ+ rights. There is a difference, however, between taking issue with Israel's housing policy in East Jerusalem and accusing Israel of "stealing" Palestinian land. The former is legitimate grounds for debate; the latter is untrue and an incarnation of an age-old antisemitic trope about "greedy, thieving Jews."

A central thesis here is that *demonizing* Israel is antisemitic. This should not and does not preclude good-faith debate on specific Israeli policies. Or specific Israeli politicians. If that were the case, all nine million Israeli citizens would have nothing to talk about. I do not discuss a wide range of Israeli policies or politics because they are not relevant to my thesis. It does not matter if you love former Israeli Prime Minister Benjamin Netanyahu or despise him; it still holds true that it is morally wrong to foment Jew-hatred.

It is not my intention to cover the entire scope of the Boycott, Divestment, and Sanctions campaign in depth. The purpose of this book is to educate others about the cultural boycott effort, the newest and potentially most dangerous facet of the BDS campaign because it is attacking artists of all kinds and hijacking their names and likenesses to spread anti-Israel and anti-Jewish propaganda to billions of people.

Artists who refuse to shun Israel, such as the Rolling Stones, J. K. Rowling, Paul McCartney, and Morgan Freeman, are harassed, bullied, and even physically threatened. Israeli artists face discrimination, denigration, and chants of "Kill the Jew."

Why should you care about them? You may think to yourself that of all the outrages in the world, the harm done to wealthy celebrities is low on most people's lists. To discount the personal pain these artists feel because of their professional success, however, is to discount their humanity. And as you will learn later in these pages, BDS does not just target famous artists but lesser-known and struggling artists as well. More importantly, the cultural boycott campaign against Israel is not just an attack on artists and Israel but Jews everywhere. It has made artists a pawn in the spread of a dangerous ideology that affects us all.

Nothing in this book is intended to diminish the hardships of the Palestinian people. They have suffered under the hands of their Arab neighbors, many Israeli policies, and the consequences of their own decisions. And, likewise, nothing negates the religious and emotional connection other people, such as Christians and Muslims, have to the land.

Of course, Israel has made mistakes. There are no perfect nations because there are no perfect people. To the extent there are certain inequities among the different ethnic groups in Israel, I certainly agree they should be remedied. Arab Israelis often struggle with high crime rates and poor infrastructure within their communities for a variety of reasons. There are numerous Israeli nonprofits and political groups, with both Jewish and non-Jewish advocates, working to correct this disparity. The BDS campaign, which foments hostilities between the Jewish and Arab populations of the country, does nothing to further this important goal.

Jew-haters have weaponized culture, and Jews everywhere need to pay attention to this now. We are a diverse people leading different lives, but when the sky darkens with hate, to the rest of the world we look amazingly alike.

The tattoos I saw as a child are indelible reminders for me of what happens when Jew-hatred goes unchecked. I understood then and know now that Jew-hatred can grow like a fungus, even in places where we feel at home. It ebbs and rises, but like the undertow of the ocean, antisemitism will always lie beneath the surface—powerful and ominous—unless we recognize and reject it in all its forms.

In 2011, I took up arms against the cultural boycott campaign and joined a fledgling entertainment-based nonprofit called Creative Community for Peace (CCFP), where I served as its first director. This position gave me a unique opportunity to counter the cultural boycott campaign against Israel as well as analyze its development.

Hundreds of artists and musicians book visits and concert dates in Israel each year, and nearly all of them are pressured to cancel. To bolster their resolve, I contacted the people they trust—their representatives. I educated them about Israel and dispelled the disinformation they were receiving. I made them aware of what to expect from the boycott campaign, listened to their concerns, answered their questions, and was successful in averting many potential cancelations. I corresponded with the heads of media, communications, and television network companies when their upcoming events or news coverage appeared likely to give unbalanced coverage to BDS propaganda. Then and since, I have witnessed ugly social media wars, followed countless news stories, and written on this topic in international publications.

In 2015, I created Liberate Art to take the fight to the next level and educate a wider audience about the goals, strategies, and tactics of the cultural boycott campaign and its poisonous impact on art and audiences everywhere. Liberate Art has worked with student groups, religious institutions, entertainment groups, entertainment industry publications, corporations, and leaders in Israel advocacy in Los Angeles, New York, Boston, Paris, London, and Jerusalem.

In addition, Liberate Art creates unique platforms for international artists to express their support for Israel. We brought eight-time Grammy winner Ziggy Marley together with the Jewish National Fund (JNF) in support of its clean water initiative. We produced the first anti-BDS celebrity panel, with artists from film, television, and music, including musician Alan Parsons (the Alan Parsons Project) and the iconic writer/director/producer David Zucker (his credits include *Airplane!*, *The Naked Gun*, *Scary Movie 4*, and *Scary Movie 5*).

I am often asked to be a guest on TV and talk radio shows to lend my expertise on the topic. As a result, I have discovered that many people, even the best-informed members of the pro-Israel community, do not really understand the cultural boycott campaign: how it works, which artists support it, why it is so dangerous, and how to talk about it.

This book will educate and empower them.

CHAPTER ONE

SCARLETT JOHANSSON AND SODASTREAM

"I remain a supporter of economic cooperation and social interaction between a democratic Israel and Palestine."

—SCARLETT JOHANSSON, AMERICAN ACTRESS

When Scarlett Johansson signed up to be the spokesperson for Israeli soft-drink machine maker SodaStream, she did not know what she was in for.

She did not expect social media memes to circulate with a scarlet "A" for apartheid carved into her forehead. She did not know her representatives would be flooded with emails and phone calls accusing her of crimes against humanity or that traditional and digital media would spread that lie to millions of people across the globe. She never imagined a seven-year relationship with an international nonprofit would end in a public divorce. She did not suspect proponents of the BDS campaign against

Israel would be determined to bring the SodaStream plant down, and her along with it.

In 2005, the world-famous actress began a decade of service as a global ambassador for Oxfam, the UK-based charity that seeks to end global poverty. In 2013, she agreed to become the spokesperson for SodaStream International Ltd., a corporation with hundreds of millions of dollars in annual revenue. The two ventures came to loggerheads before Super Bowl Sunday 2014.

SodaStream and Johansson were a perfect match: SodaStream features reusable devices that transform ordinary tap water into carbonated soft drinks and sparkling water in reusable, environmentally friendly bottles, and the actress, a well-known environmental activist, had been using the product, which she loved, for years.

Johansson also admired that SodaStream, a progressive Israeli company, had built a factory that was a model of peaceful cooperation between Israelis and Palestinians. The factory employed 1,100 workers—mostly West Bank Palestinians—who all enjoyed the same conditions and salaries whether Jewish or Palestinian.[1]

When SodaStream trumpeted the association and plans for a thirty-second ad during one of the most-watched events on the planet—the Super Bowl—it set off a vitriolic attack against both the movie star and the company. SodaStream had long been in the crosshairs of BDS because one of its factories was near Ma'aleh Adumim, a Jerusalem suburb in the West Bank, and any Jewish presence in land sought for a future Palestinian state is hotly protested by BDS advocates.

I had been the director at CCFP for several years, and I knew what was coming down the pike. With BDS involved, it was going to be a media massacre. I reached out to Johansson's publicist, Marcel Pariseau, at True Public Relations. In my mind, my goal was twofold: first, prepare them for the fallout that was sure to follow, and second, helm a proactive response to the mayhem. What ensued was many late-night conversations and emails. I had a definite sense that Johansson would not be bullied, and although Pariseau was educating and counseling her, she was calling all the shots.

The BDS-manufactured "controversy" flooded newspapers, magazines, TV, and the internet. Graphic images of Johansson and "blood bubbles" swarmed social media. BDS supporters claimed that her association with the Israeli company made her complicit in supposed crimes against humanity. Roger Waters, co-founder of Pink Floyd and a celebrity leader of the movement, insinuated that she was naïve and lacked strength and integrity.[2]

Oxfam weighed in, posting the following below Johansson's bio on its website: "Oxfam believes that businesses that operate in settlements further the ongoing poverty and denial of rights of the Palestinian communities that we work to support. Oxfam is opposed to all trade from Israeli settlements."[3] Although the IRS bans political campaign activity by charities, a threat hung in the air. Would Oxfam drop Johansson because of her association with SodaStream?

Johansson defended her association with the Israeli company, saying, "SodaStream is a company that is not only committed to the environment but to building a bridge to peace between

Israel and Palestine, supporting neighbors working alongside each other, receiving equal pay, equal benefits, and equal rights."[4]

Thousands of individuals, as well as organizations in Hollywood and beyond, wanted to show their support for Johansson and SodaStream, so I organized a "gratitude campaign," ultimately delivering thousands of "thank you" notes from her fans to her through her publicist.

In the end, it was Scarlett who ended the relationship with Oxfam, saying the two "have a fundamental difference of opinion in regards to the Boycott, Divestment, and Sanctions movement."[5]

Bowing to BDS cost Oxfam greatly. Numerous Oxfam supporters disagreed with its stance on Israel and its public politicking. Chief Executive Mark Goldring later confessed that the Johansson furor was "something of a PR disaster" for the organization and cost Oxfam America "literally thousands of donors."[6]

BDS's attacks on SodaStream did not harm the company, but they did affect the Palestinian workers there. SodaStream eventually decided to close its plant in the West Bank, and as a result, five hundred Palestinians lost their jobs.[7] If BDS proponents were truly concerned about the welfare of Palestinians, they would reexamine this strategy; they have not.

SodaStream has since opened another plant in southern Israel. The plant provides employment for around 1,400 workers, many of them Negev Bedouins. Naturally, BDS wants the new facility boycotted as well.[8]

There are hundreds of stories like Scarlett Johansson's happening every year as the Boycott, Sanctions, and Divestment campaign places artists in the crosshairs of its war against Israel.

NEXT STEP: INCREASE YOUR AWARENESS.

Hundreds of artists are attacked every year for visiting or associating with Israel.

Follow me on social media and sign up for Liberate Art's newsletters for the latest news and action opportunities.

Website: www.LiberateArt.net

Facebook: www.facebook.com/LiberateArt

Twitter: https://twitter.com/LanaMelman

Newsletter sign up: www.LiberateArt.net

Instagram: https://www.instagram.com/Lana.Melman/

CHAPTER TWO

THE POWER OF THE ARTS AND ARTISTS

"[The Beatles] are more popular than Jesus now."
—JOHN LENNON, BRITISH MUSICIAN-SONGWRITER, 1966

Artists influence the world and foster change through the art they create and the stories they tell—engaging us, educating us, and rousing our emotions. They help create bridges between people and cultures. They are role models for fashion and social norms. They can draw attention to social and political causes and create social change through their celebrity. And their celebrity can be used by third parties to drum up support for their own political agendas. The BDS campaign against Israel seeks to use the celebrity of artists as a tool to destroy Israel and stir up hate against Jews worldwide.

ART HAS THE POWER TO INFLUENCE

Art transforms culture by affecting individuals. Dalton Trumbo's anti-war novel *Johnny Got His Gun,* written decades before my birth, indelibly altered my perception of war. The 1939 novel is a stream-of-consciousness study of a soldier during World War I. In the narrative, his mind is functioning perfectly, but he slowly comes to realize he is in a hospital bed, and an exploding artillery shell cost him his arms, legs, and face. A husk of the man he once was, the soldier has only one thing left: his thoughts. His first instinct is to try to kill himself, but war has rendered him powerless to end his own life. Blind, deaf, and mute, he struggles to communicate with the outside world. He frantically taps out messages in Morse code by banging his head against his mattress, hoping someone will understand he is reaching out. He wants his life to have meaning. He wants his body to be placed in a glass box and toured around the country to show the world the true horrors of war. Finally, a nurse realizes he is trying to talk to her, and his military superiors are summoned to hear his wish. But will the military establishment let the world see the ravages its wars leave behind? No; it is clear to the reader this soldier is condemned to live out the rest of his natural life in his semi-living hell.

There are few among us who have not been moved, enlightened, or influenced by the art we experience. The arts can create a window into lives we might not otherwise know and create empathy for people we previously thought very different from ourselves. They can memorialize an entire movement or stir emotion around a public event. And they can also be a catalyst for dramatic social change.

ROLE MODELS

In addition to influencing the world through their art, with fame, artists can serve as role models for society.

In 1966, at the height of the Beatles's popularity, John Lennon remarked in an interview for the British newspaper the *Evening Standard* that the group was "more popular than Jesus." He did not mean the band was better than Jesus but rather they were more influential on the younger generation. And he might have been right. The legendary English rock band from Liverpool influenced hairstyles, fashion, and music and normalized recreational drug use. The Beatles's trips to India brought the sitar into Western music. Yoga, meditation, and psychedelic-drug use boomed in the United States.

Madonna was at one point the best-selling female recording artist of all time[9] and is regarded as one of the most influential personalities in pop culture ever.[10] In the 1980s, she put herself forward as a role model, breaking taboos regarding sexual preference, interracial love, foreign adoptions, and blended families, as well as an icon of female empowerment.

Hip-hop music, pioneered by African American and Hispanic youth in New York's South Bronx in the 1970s and legends such as Tupac Shakur in California in the 1990s, continues to have a dramatic impact on teens, particularly Black youth, influencing everything from fashion to worldview with its universal themes of social justice and the search for identity.

Of course, these few cases are just by way of example; the list is endless.

SOCIAL ADVOCATES

And then, there is celebrity political advocacy. Fiery soapbox rhetoric is popular among many artists who wish to make a difference in the world. They may influence the thinking of some while simply dismaying others, but they do, undeniably, draw attention to causes with their comments and actions.

Artists will speak at protest marches and campaign events and engage in heated social media debates. Their activism draws crowds and makes news. Whether they are trying to tilt the country and the world in the right direction is subjective and depends on your politics and worldview. The question is: do they make a real impact?

Sometimes, artists and entertainers draw considerable attention to causes most people would consider worthy without that attention translating to lasting change. Consider the case of George Clooney and Darfur. Darfur is a region of Sudan in East Africa. In 2003, a civil war erupted between the government and various tribes in Sudan, and a campaign of ethnic cleansing killed thousands of non-Arab Sudanese. Starting in 2006, Clooney traveled to Darfur, raised money, and even addressed the United Nations (UN) about the atrocities committed there. In 2010, he started an organization, the Satellite Sentinel Project, to document human rights abuses in the country. In 2012, Clooney was arrested[11] during a protest outside Sudan's embassy in Washington, D.C.*

In 2014, an article in the British newspaper *The Guardian* investigated whether there seemed to be a lasting impact on the situation there. They interviewed aid workers; the president of the Sudanese Development Initiative; the founding director of the Enough Project, which fights to end genocide; and several

---

* He posted and forfeited a $100 bond, resolving the matter.

other non-governmental organization (NGO) leaders. Sadly, the investigation concluded that, although Clooney had brought sizable attention to the crisis in the region, there was no lasting impact from his advocacy, and the situation there today is as bad as or worse than it was before Clooney's intervention.[12]

Then, there was the 2016 presidential election in the United States. Although much of Hollywood turned out for Hillary Clinton, their support did not impact the outcome of the election, and the former senator and first lady lost to Donald Trump, who was widely reviled in La La Land.

On the other hand, with the Me Too Movement, artists were instrumental in changing America's attitude toward sexual intimidation in the workplace. The phrase "MeToo" was first used on social media (Myspace, specifically) in 2006 by Tarana Burke, a sexual harassment survivor, as a way for young, vulnerable women to share their stories and empathize with others who'd had similar experiences. In 2017, actress Alyssa Milano encouraged the use of the phrase as a hashtag (#MeToo) following multiple allegations of sexual abuse by producer Harvey Weinstein and posted a call for women who had been victims of sexual harassment and sexual abuse to change their social media status to "Me Too." This prompted dozens of celebrity posts and testimonials from actresses and other performers, including Gwyneth Paltrow,[13] Angelina Jolie,[14] Rose McGowan,[15] Ashley Judd,[16] and Uma Thurman.[17]

These famous women triggered an outpouring from women all over the world, the great majority of whom were not celebrities, who spoke their truth and shared their stories. Weinstein was eventually charged and convicted of sexual abuse and is now in prison. The social movement created pressure on entertainment companies to act. Other previously powerful men in Hollywood were accused of sexual harassment, sexual abuse, or inappropriate behavior (accusations that were often denied), and some were fired and/or shunned within the industry, including *Today* anchor Matt Lauer, hip-hop artist R. Kelly, talk-show hosts Charlie Rose and Tavis Smiley, actor Kevin Spacey, and comic Louis C.K. The Me Too Movement was also a catalyst for policy changes throughout corporate America, including rendering unenforceable non-disclosure agreements tied to sexual harassment settlements and ending the practice of paying sexual predators large sums to leave companies. The Me Too Movement has spread to countries throughout the world, including Britain, France, India, and Ukraine, among many others.

Today, musician and BDS front man Roger Waters is using his stardom and influence to—in my opinion—wreak political havoc and, on a darker level, propagate Jew-hatred. His "cause" does not favor a positive evolution for a better world but rather the perpetuation of an ancient hate.

Waters and his followers are pushing for a cultural boycott of Israel and Israeli artists. They want international artists to shun performances in Israel and international venues to rescind invitations to Israeli artists. Their rhetoric reeks of classic antisemitic tropes, demonizes Israel, and is stirring up Jew-hatred worldwide.

In his shows, Waters has toted a machine-gun replica while wearing a long, black, leather coat and armband reminiscent of a Nazi uniform[18] and shown a video of B-52s dropping bombs in the shapes of Jewish stars, US dollars, and corporate symbols. Waters has compared Israel to apartheid South Africa and its government to the Third Reich and—in one home video—extraterrestrial aliens.[19] He has accused Israelis of crimes against humanity too numerous to mention. He has disparaged the Jewish homeland in interviews, opinion pieces, public speaking engagements, concerts, and at the United Nations. What began as a personal political opinion has morphed into what might be called an obsession and has become a crusade.

In a 2013 *Rolling Stone* interview, Waters issued a call to his fellow artists to boycott the Jewish state. Like a hall monitor from hell, he polices the decisions of other artists, finding them at fault for wanting to play for their Israeli fans. He has called singer Nick Cave, formerly of Nick Cave and the Bad Seeds, arrogant and indifferent and Thom Yorke, of Radiohead, whiny and detached.[20] In a blog post on Salon.com, he called American singer Dionne Warwick profoundly ignorant and disingenuous for her decision to perform in Israel.[21] It got more than eighty-four thousand Facebook shares.

These verbal attacks by Waters on other artists bring widespread attention to the "cause." As Nick Cave opined, musicians who perform in Israel are now forced to "go through public humiliation from Roger Waters."

At Waters's concert in Belgium in July 2013, a giant, pig-shaped balloon emblazoned with the Jewish Star of David was released into the sky to float above the crowd.[22] The Simon Wiesenthal Center included this incident in its 2013 list of "Top Ten Anti-Semitic/Anti-Israel Slurs,"[23] listing Waters with such paragons of Jew-hatred as Iran's Ayatollah Khamenei.

HOW BDS USES THE CELEBRITY OF ARTISTS

Currently, very few artists support the cultural boycott campaign, but BDS is seeking converts by any means possible.

Whereas most causes and political campaigns search out like-minded artists to advocate on their behalf, BDS attacks artists who do not share its ideology and attempts to browbeat them into submission. It seeks to "convert" artists through demagoguery (lying for emotional effect and scapegoating Israel) and public shaming (attacking cultural exchange with Israel as immoral).

When an artist books a trip to (or concert date in) Israel, BDS groups pressure him or her to cancel. They claim anyone wanting to perform for their Israeli fans is giving a "stamp of approval" to the colonialism, apartheid, oppression, and ethnic cleansing BDS falsely claims Israel promulgates. They circulate deceptive statements, letters, and petitions on Facebook, Twitter, and Instagram, which often go viral. BDS seeks to intimidate, not educate, waving the cancellation guillotine over any errant artist's neck.

Artists are public figures who need audience support to succeed, making them particularly vulnerable to attacks on their character. When BDS accuses them of hypocrisy or aligning with human rights violators, it is a direct and very public assault on their reputations and therefore on their livelihoods. It can take ten seconds for someone to soil your name and a lifetime for you to redeem it.

The cultural boycott looks to exploit the desire of artists to avoid public shaming. It wants artists to be afraid that if they refuse to boycott Israel, they will be embroiled in a controversy, and the false charges against them will stick like chewing gum on the bottom of one's shoe.

George Clooney and Alyssa Milano are, or were, thought leaders (whether you agree with them or not) who publicly embraced causes they personally believed in, whereas, as you will see later in this book, artists like Lana Del Rey, Lorde, and Demi Lovato canceled concert dates in Israel and parroted BDS rhetoric only after extensive bullying and intimidation.

BDS promotes as role models the minority of artists who do support the boycott. It also misrepresents as advocates artists who were bullied into canceling visits to Israel or simply desired to avoid the controversy. The objective is to create the illusion of a movement in hopes that both the public and other artists will follow suit.

BDS, however, does not need to change the minds of artists to benefit from their celebrity.

Anti-Israel agitators have realized that if they can create controversy around a celebrity by accusing them of supporting apartheid, they can get news outlets to carry the story and create social media buzz. And when publications run stories about artists attacked for performing in Israel, the lies, misinformation, and mischaracterizations about the Jewish homeland appear in the story as well.

NEXT STEP: RECOGNIZE THE THREAT.

Recognize the cultural boycott campaign as a serious threat to Israel and Jews worldwide.

CHAPTER THREE

ANTIZIONISM IS
ANTISEMITISM

*"I remember my dad frankly telling me, 'People
hate Jews. Just be aware of that. They just do.'"*

—SETH ROGEN, CANADIAN ACTOR

Antisemitism is not new. Loosely defined as hatred or hostility
toward Jews, it dates nearly as far back as Jewish history itself,
having existed in the ancient empires of Babylonia, Greece, and
Rome.

The Nazi Holocaust may be history's most extreme and well-
documented (although frequently minimized or denied)
example of antisemitism, but there are countless other cases. In
Medieval Europe, Jews were denied citizenship and civil liber-
ties and suffered intermittent spells of forced conversion, mass
expulsion, and mass murder. Jews were expelled from England in
1290, from France in 1306, and from Portugal and Spain in 1492.

Thousands of Jews, as well as Muslims, died at the hands of the

Christians during the Crusades. Millions of Jews were killed during the Spanish Inquisition, in the aftermath of the Russian Revolution, and in the pogroms throughout Europe, where the local non-Jewish population killed their Jewish neighbors, often aided by government and police forces. The Cossack rebels of Ukraine burned Jewish villages to the ground, raped their women, and killed their men. Centuries of anti-Jewish discrimination and violence in Arab countries are well documented by Ben-Dror Yemini in his book *Industry of Lies*.*

In fact, antisemitism is systemic and institutionalized worldwide. It has endured for millennia and across continents. The late Lord Jonathan Sacks, former Chief Rabbi of the United Hebrew Congregations of the Commonwealth, posited that Jews were hated in the Middle Ages for their religion, in the nineteenth and twentieth centuries for their race, and today for their state.[24]

We are told antizionism is about Israel, but in fact, it is an attack on Jews—and many Jews either do not see that or are bullied into not accepting what they see.

---

* In the twentieth century, Nazi Germany, led by Adolf Hitler, who was first elected chancellor in 1933 and then führer in 1934, exterminated six million Jews, including a million children. Jewish citizens in Europe were arrested, aggregated in ghettos, forced onto cattle cars, and taken by train to thousands of forced labor camps, as well as to the extermination camps of Belzec, Sobibor, Treblinka, and Auschwitz-Birkenau, where they were starved, tortured, and murdered. At Treblinka, during the peak of its operation in 1942, some fifteen thousand innocent Jewish men, women, and children were murdered every day, most within two hours of their arrival. They were forced to leave their belongings and take off their clothes. Their hair was then shaved off, after which they were forced under beatings to run up a path to a bathhouse, where they were herded into chambers and gassed in little more than twenty minutes. Jewish workers were then forced to remove their bodies, extract gold and silver fillings from their teeth, and then carry the corpses to large pits, where the bodies were incinerated in big fires. In little more than a year, more than 870,000 Jews were murdered in this one location, the ashes from the "ovens" piled on the side of the road to the entrance like snow.

Antizionism is antisemitism. It traffics in modern-day blood libel (the false allegation that Jews murder Christians during their rituals) and anti-Jewish conspiracy theories about money and power. It demonizes Israel and creates an environment that makes Jew-hatred more acceptable worldwide. And it singles out the Jewish homeland for criticism and reproach disproportionate to its errors.

Today, BDS and its progressive friends are forcing many Jews to choose between supporting Israel, which for many is part of their ethnicity or faith, and the liberal causes they care about.[25] As English comic and author David Baddiel asserts, non-Israeli Jews are expected to "feel a bit ashamed of Israel, and must, before they are allowed into any kind of public conversation, make some kind of supplicant-like statement to that effect."[26]

Appallingly, classic antisemitism is regarded by many as second-class racism unworthy of moral outrage. Even worse, the Jew-hatred inside antizionism is not readily recognized because it has been normalized and falsely justified. The BDS campaign has tapped into the almost primal nature of Jew-hatred to convince many that supporting antizionism places them on the right side of history.

Numerous polls conducted in recent years have shown a direct correlation between antizionism and antisemitism, with large segments of the population echoing the false accusations circulated by BDS. An Action and Protection League (APL) poll collected five hundred thousand data points from a total of sixteen thousand people in sixteen EU countries from December 2019 to January 2020. One-fourth of those polled equated Israelis to Nazis and agreed that this justifies an international boycott of Israel. One-fifth of those polled said they "strongly agree" or "tend to agree" that it is always better to be a little cautious with Jews, and 21 percent expressed their belief that "there is a secret Jewish network that influences political and economic affairs in the world." Clearly, behavior follows perception, as the data also showed an increase in the number of antisemitic incidents in the United Kingdom, the Netherlands, France, and Austria.[27]

This should be of concern to non-Jews also. Why? Because antisemitism is a human problem, an illiberal ideology that undermines pluralism and tolerance, and a virus that destroys societies and souls.

RISING ANTISEMITISM AND ANTIZIONISM IN THE ENTERTAINMENT INDUSTRY

Outside of rap music, which is singular in its provocative and often antagonistic lyrics directed toward a wide spectrum of groups, including women and gays as well as Jews, I rarely witnessed an outward expression of classic antisemitism in my twenty-plus years working in the entertainment business.

When Mel Gibson was arrested for drunk driving in 2006 and, according to the police report, blurted out a barrage of antisemitic remarks about the "f*****g Jews" saying, "The Jews are responsible for all the wars in the world,"* members of the entertainment industry, along with the rest of the country, were

---

* "Gibson Charged with Drunken Driving," *CNN*, August 3, 2006, https://www.cnn.com/2006/LAW/08/02/gibson.charged/index.html; Gibson later said the words were "blurted out in a moment of insanity" and apologized to the Jewish community. The DUI conviction was subsequently expunged, as often happens with first-time offenders.

shocked by his comments. Antizionism, on the other hand, has been slowly rising since the start of the cultural boycott campaign in 2005.

Both classic antisemitism and antizionism in the entertainment industry, however, exploded in 2020 during the COVID-19 pandemic and the summer of protests that divided our nation. There are two main reasons for this: first, Jew-hatred wanes during times of prosperity but inevitably flows during chaos and unrest; and second, fifteen years of the BDS movement describing the Jews of Israel as monsters had normalized and even legitimized this perversion.

BDS entangles the ideas of the bad Jew and the bad Israeli and provides artists—and others—with the language and ideas of classic antisemitism when it criticizes the Jewish state. When BDS proponents or others vilify Israelis, they are not referring to the Arab citizens who make up 20 percent of the population; they are talking about the Jews.

While artists such as Jon Stewart, Halsey, John Oliver, Mia Farrow, Viola Davis, and Mark Ruffalo do not (to date) explicitly call for a cultural boycott of Israel, they till the soil for the BDS campaign by demonizing Israel. I refer to these antizionist artists as "Israel Bashers." While some of them would strongly deny their thoughts or hearts are antisemitic, to me, their comments clearly are. As you will see, antizionism among artists is not black and white; it comes in shades of gray.

Some Israel Bashers do not make any attempt to disguise their contempt for the Jewish homeland. Examples, in my opinion, include fashion icons Gigi and Bella Hadid, whose father is a wealthy Beverly Hills hotelier of Palestinian descent, and English singer Dua Lipa, who is dating Gigi's and Bella's brother Anwar Hadid.[28] When the Hadid sisters, with their combined Instagram reach of 119 million followers (a number that dwarfs Israel's 6.6 million Jews), disseminate disinformation about the Jewish homeland, it has a significant impact on the perception of Israel around the world.

Although some Israel Bashers believe their condemnation of Israel is unbiased criticism, it lacks balance and objectivity. There is no sign of empathy for the suffering of innocent Israelis or any criticism of Hamas's goal to destroy the Jewish state or the militant organization's reign of terror on both Israelis and its own people. These artists are entitled to their opinions, but as public figures with outsized microphones, they have an obligation to get the story straight. If they spent thirty minutes reading Hamas's charter, with its pledge to destroy Israel, or researching how it treats homosexuals and regards women and contrasted that to the rights of gays, women, and minorities in Israel, they might be moved to treat all the players with a fair hand.

NEXT STEP: NAME IT.

It is ironic that people still debate the meaning of the term "antisemitism" after thousands of years of anti-Jewish discrimination.

The term "Jew-hatred" is powerful and clear. Use it.

CHAPTER FOUR

ANTISEMITIC LIES

*"If there's one thing Jewish people have
showed us, it's they have the power."*

—CHARLAMAGNE THA GOD, AMERICAN
RADIO AND TV PERSONALITY

The persecution and murder of Jews always begins with the propagation of vicious calumnies and conspiracy theories commonly referred to as "antisemitic tropes." Many people, especially Jews, are quick to recognize these tropes when they are directed at Jews in general ("classic antisemitism") but either fail to recognize them or rationalize them away when they are directed at Israel ("antizionism"). The latter, however, is no less dangerous to Jews than the former, and both need to be recognized and called out by everyone.

You can see the fluid relationship between antisemitism and antizionism in the examples below.

LIE #1: JEWS ARE EVIL

In her book *How to Fight Anti-Semitism,* former *New York Times* editor Bari Weiss describes antisemitism as an ideology that is ever-morphing yet always the same. At every time in history and every place in the world where antisemitism has reared its head, Jews (and/or the Jewish state) have been accused of being evil.

What is considered evil may change from generation to generation, but the group falsely accused of being behind it never does.* Jews have been condemned both for being capitalists and for being communists. They have been demonized for being too white and not white enough. Today, when racism and colonialism are roundly denounced throughout the Western world, voices from the left are accusing Israel of apartheid and land theft. Jews are not just falsely accused of bad deeds but blackened hearts. Israeli soldiers are described as depraved and Israel's government as genocidal.

In 2006, when Mel Gibson claimed Jews were responsible for all the world's wars or in 2020 when American rapper Ice Cube combined the Star of David with demonic images on his Instagram feed, it was easy to recognize these as the classic antisemitic trope about evil Jews. But how is that different from American songstress Halsey seemingly calling the Israelis racists when she says "brown children are being murdered" on Twitter in 2021?[29]

The Israeli–Palestinian conflict is not about skin color! Fewer than half of the Jews in Israel are of Russian or European

---

* Including, of course, perhaps the most destructive accusation of all—killing God in the form of Jesus Christ.

descent, and all Jews can trace their lineage back to the Middle East. It seems to me, Halsey is either ignorant of these facts or ignores them. Either way, the fallacious white/brown dichotomy plays on today's fiery racial tensions and decidedly leans on the antisemitic trope of the evil (in this case racist) Jew.

LIE #2: JEWS ARE BLOODTHIRSTY

The term "blood libel" was originally coined to describe the accusation of ritualist murder of Christian children by Jews, but the term quickly came to refer to all unfounded accusations of Jews murdering innocent people, including by poisoning wells and spreading disease.

Today, we regard the Middle Ages accusations that Jews were responsible for the Black Plague and poisoning wells as, well, medieval. In the wake of the COVID-19 pandemic in the twenty-first century, however, without a shred of evidence, thousands of people on social media pointed to Israel as the source of the virus—although the overwhelming majority of scientists believe it originated in mainland China—or accused the Jewish state of withholding a cure. The hashtag #Covid1948 ("1948" being the date of Israel's founding and the implication being the Israelis were responsible for the disease) spread like wildfire.

Swept up in the furor, American actress Rosanna Arquette claimed that Israel already had a vaccine but was delaying distribution of the life-saving medicine to the world for financial gain. Her now-deleted Twitter post read that Israel "has been working on a corona virus vaccine for a year already" and has put "lives at risk for profit" by supposedly refusing to release it. The actress, who is Jewish, subsequently apologized, saying she was "confused."[30]

Just as COVID-19 vaccinations were beginning to save lives in 2021, *Saturday Night Live*'s Michael Che made the following joke in the "Weekend Update" portion of *SNL*: "Israel is reporting that they've vaccinated half of their population. I'm going to guess it's the Jewish half."[31]

First, let me say that I think comedy is slowly being snuffed out today by "wokeness," and that is unfortunate for all of us. I do not believe all ethnic humor is bad. Ethnic humor has its place when it is recognized as true by the group it is referring to and that group thinks it is funny. Michael Che's so-called joke was based on a lie that was then making the rounds on social media that Israel was withholding this life-saving medication from its non-Jewish population.

In truth, all of Israel's citizens and residents were eligible for this vaccine regardless of ethnicity or religion. By alleging that the Jewish homeland withheld vaccinations from its Arab citizens, Che's "joke" promotes the blood libel trope that Jews are advancing the spread of disease.

The lie about Jews murdering children has been given new momentum by Israel Bashers. In 2020, Dua Lipa shared a post with her 76 million followers on Instagram that blamed Israel for creating Hamas and said in part, "The big bad tough guys of the #IDF thoroughly enjoy beating and shooting children. They even have shirts that depict a pregnant Palestinian woman with a sniper scope on her stomach that reads '1 shot two kills.' But don't worry," the post continued, "they're all terrorist, so it's all good. We totally understand." Following a backlash, the three-time Grammy winner retreated and deleted the post.[32]

When Israel defended itself against missiles shot at its citizens in 2021, actress Mia Farrow posted a photo[33] of herself with her arm around three Gazan children paired with an image of a war-torn building. The caption read "Kids in Gaza"—arguably an unsubtle message that Israel was killing Palestinian children.

LIES #3 AND #4: JEWS ARE GREEDY AND ALL-POWERFUL

The trope about Jews and money (the stereotypic greedy Jew who cheats and steals) and the lie about the all-powerful Jews who control the world in dark and sinister ways are other mainstays of both classic antisemitism and antizionism. These lies were codified in the false and defamatory fabrication called *The Protocols of the Elders of Zion (The Protocols)*, first published in Russia in 1903.[34]

The Nazi Party disseminated *The Protocols* to drum up distrust and hate in the hearts of the German people and set the stage for the horrors of the Holocaust. In the United States, Henry Ford, founder of the Ford Motor Company, translated, published, and distributed five hundred thousand copies of the text in his widely read newspaper the *Dearborn Independent* in the 1920s.[35] It has been endorsed by Arab leaders in Iraq, Egypt, and Saudi Arabia,[36] and a reference to *The Protocols* appears in the 1988 charter of the terrorist organization Hamas.[37]

These lies trace their origins to the Middle Ages, when Jews could not own land and were prohibited from participating in numerous professions. As a practical matter, Jews were limited to being merchants or involved in businesses frowned upon by the general population, such as moneylending, which was viewed as not Christian (Jesus spoke out against the moneylenders at the Temple). Their experience as moneylenders gave them a foothold into a profession that *was* open to them—banking. Their debtors characterized the Jewish lenders as avaricious, greedy, corrupt, and exploitative, when usually they were just collecting the debts owed to them or others.

Beyond supposedly controlling the world's financial markets and banking systems, the Jews are also regularly accused of controlling the media. While it is true that Jews have participated in news media and Hollywood in greater numbers than their percentage among the general population, once again, this is because journalism and the entertainment industry were nontraditional occupations open to them. Whatever past ownership may have been, today media companies are international conglomerates that are, for the most part, public companies. However, numerous artists are now proliferating these antisemitic tropes in their song lyrics and public comments directed at both Israel and Jews at large.

In 2020, actor, director, rapper, and TV host Nick Cannon propagated classic antisemitic tropes about Jewish money and power in an episode of his podcast *Cannon's Class*, where he talked about "going as deep as the Rothschilds,* centralized banking, the 13 families, the bloodlines that control everything even outside of America."[38]

---

* The Rothschild family is a wealthy, Jewish banking family originally from Frankfurt, Germany. The family patriarch started the business in the 1760s, and his five sons grew it internationally, establishing branches in London, Paris, Frankfurt, Vienna, and Naples. The expression "the Rothschilds" is a dog whistle for the antisemitic trope regarding Jewish money and power.

When Cannon initially lost his job at ViacomCBS for his remarks (they rehired him a few months later),[39] American radio presenter and television personality Charlamagne Tha God blamed the "Jewish people" who "have the power" in the media for the firing. "Listen, Nick is my guy," Charlamagne said during the broadcast of his radio show *The Breakfast Club*. "I hate it had to be him, but that's what you can do when you have the power. And if there's one thing Jewish people have showed us, it's they have the power."[40]

Nick Cannon has since retracted and apologized for his comments. He has worked with Jewish leaders, including Malcolm Hoenlein, Executive Vice Chairman of the Conference of Presidents of Major American Jewish Organizations, and been an outspoken advocate for Holocaust education. In my 2020 exclusive interview with the TV host, Cannon said it was "time to end Jew-hatred" and that he is "determined to change a negative experience into a positive one and help to end any type of discrimination and hatred."[41]

In the same year, Rapper Ice Cube landed in the middle of a Twitter storm with a series of memes on social media. One of those memes, originally a London public mural that has since been taken down, depicted what many viewed as stereotyped Jewish bankers playing Monopoly on the backs of brown-skinned people. The image was captioned, "All we have to do is stand up and their little game is over."[42] When confronted about the antisemitic trope, Ice Cube replied that it was his "truth."[43] Twitter responded with a tepid wrist slap, saying the post "might contain sensitive content."[44]

Unlike numerous celebrities and others who have fallen like

dominoes because of errant remarks against women and non-Jewish minorities, most celebrities who make comments like Ice Cube's are not threatened by loss of employment (Nick Cannon is one of the exceptions), leading Joshua Malina, the *West Wing* and *Scandal* star, to query, "Why's it so hard to get cancel culture on the line when the problem is antisemitism?"[45]

NBA legend Kareem Abdul-Jabbar called out Ice Cube and others for their antisemitic comments in a column for the *Hollywood Reporter*, complaining that hate speech against Jews typically goes unpunished. "If we're going to be outraged by injustice," he wrote, "let's be outraged by injustice against anyone."[46]

Instead of apologizing, however, Ice Cube doubled down with another trope, saying, "Shame on the *Hollywood Reporter* who obviously gave my brother Kareem 30 pieces of silver to cut us down without even a phone call."* [47]

The antisemitic lies about Jews controlling the purse strings of the world extend to Israel as well. After the United Arab Emirates (UAE) and Israel signed a historic peace deal called the Abraham Accords, American record producer Farid Nassar, a.k.a. "Fredwreck," who has produced albums for big-name artists such as Eminem, Britney Spears, and Ice Cube, disseminated this same trope, only this time throwing in bit of antizionism, saying, "The Shekel is the new God. #freepalestine."[48]

In 2019, American actor and liberal activist John Cusack retweeted a cartoon depicting Jewish power—a giant hand adorned with a Jewish star squashing a group of tiny people beneath it. The

---

* Thirty pieces of silver is the price for which the Jewish Judas Iscariot betrayed Jesus, according to an account in the Gospel of Matthew 26:15 in the New Testament.

cartoon included a quote falsely attributed to Voltaire, "To learn who rules over you, simply find out who you are not allowed to criticize," and Cusack added, "Follow the money."[49] In fact, the quote is a reworking of one by Kevin Alfred Strom, an American white nationalist and Holocaust denier. There was immediate backlash against both the authorship error and Cusack's blatant antisemitism. His defense, ironically, was, as author Bari Weiss put it, "I didn't think 'Jews' when I saw it...all I thought was 'Israel.'"[50]

In the midst of the 2021 Israel–Gaza conflict, Pakistani actress Veena Malik brought all this classic antisemitism and antizionism to its logical conclusion when she expressed her desire for the world to be rid of Israel with a quote she falsely attributed to Hitler, saying: "I would have killed all the Jews of the world... but I kept some to show the world why I killed them."[51]

The notion that a historically persecuted minority controls the world is absurd. Similarly, to portray Israel as all-powerful, the way antizionists do, is to willfully ignore the reality that Israel sits by itself on a small portion of land surrounded by enemies whose lands, and populations, dwarf Israel's.

LIE #5: JEWS ARE NAZIS: ERASURE, HOLOCAUST DENIAL, AND NAZI INVERSION

"Erasure," which typically involves Holocaust denial, Nazi inversion, or the revision of Jewish history, is another example of antisemitism and has been recognized as such by the International Holocaust Remembrance Alliance (IHRA) definition adopted in 2016 and widely accepted by cities, student unions, universities, and political parties, as well as several countries, including the United States.

Thanks to the Nazi regime's systematic documentation and obsessive record-keeping and the implementation of antisemitic polices in Germany and throughout the countries under its dominion, the Holocaust is history's most well-documented campaign of Jew-hatred. In the face of this undeniable evidence, however, antisemites have turned the Nazis' Final Solution to exterminate the Jews on its head with the biggest lie of all—Holocaust denial.

Holocaust deniers call survivors "liars" and claim the crimes of the Nazis and the conditions of the Jews in the camps were exaggerated. They present themselves as "truth-seekers" and "truth-tellers" but are, in fact, the opposite. They paint the Jewish people as undeserving of sympathy for events that the deniers claim never happened.

Another form of antisemitic erasure is a revisionist theory that claims Jews are not the true Hebrews of the Bible, and the symbols, such as the star of David, have been misappropriated by them.

Richard Kylea Cowie Jr., a.k.a. Wiley, is an English rapper, songwriter, deejay, and record producer. Considered by many as the "Godfather of Grime," a genre of electronic dance music that emerged in London in the early 2000s and draws influences from jungle, dancehall, and hip-hop, he was honored as a Member of the Order of the British Empire (MBE) for his contributions to music.

In 2021, Wiley tweeted, "Listen to me Jewish community Israel is not your country I'm sorry…The Star of David that's our ting…Some people have gotten too comfortable on lands that don't belong to them." It might surprise readers to know that Wiley was not saying that the Jews stole the land of Israel from the Palestinians but rather that the Jewish homeland belongs to Black people. "Israel is ours," he added, describing his comments as the "Black History Lesson For Today."[52]

On the previously mentioned *Cannon's Class* podcast, Nick Cannon also said Black people are the "true Hebrews," and therefore, hate speech against Jews cannot possibly be antisemitic. "It's never hate speech, you can't be antisemitic when we are the Semitic people," Cannon said. "When we are the same people who they want to be. That's our birthright. We are the true Hebrews."[53]

And, finally, in what is the most perverse claim of all, BDS supporters are inordinately fond of saying that Jews, Israelis, the Israeli Defense Forces (IDF), and the State of Israel are behaving "as Nazis" themselves. In a 2014 open letter,[54] a hundred Spanish film professionals, including actors Penelope Cruz and Javier Bardem and director Pedro Almodóvar, called Israel's self-defense in the Hamas–Israeli conflict—known as Operation Protective Edge—genocide and asked the European Union to end Israel's military operation.

Nazi inversion is a mainstay of BDS and has seeped into and infected the public discourse.

NEXT STEP: QUESTION IT.

When you see or hear statements that attack Israel, ask yourself if they contain antisemitic tropes.

Become aware of how classic antisemitic tropes are being used to promote antizionism.

CHAPTER FIVE

WHAT IS BDS?

*"I was approached by different groups and political bodies
who asked me not to come here. I refused. I do what I
think, and I have many friends who support Israel."*

—PAUL MCCARTNEY, ENGLISH SINGER-SONGWRITER

Some readers may not have previously heard of BDS or, if
they have, may not be sure what it means. However, if you
have heard about the Israeli "Separation Wall" or its supposed
crimes against humanity, you have received its messaging. If
you believe that the Israeli settlements are the barrier to peace
between the Israelis and Palestinians and that Israel is an apartheid state, you have accepted some of its principles.

So, what exactly is BDS?

BDS is an acronym for "Boycott, Divestment, and Sanctions." It
is a Palestinian-led initiative meant to delegitimize and disen-
franchise the State of Israel through the intimidation of artists,
academics, and companies in the US and abroad. It seeks:

- An economic, academic, and cultural boycott of Israel.
- Divestment of financial holdings in Israeli companies and in companies that do business with Israel.
- International sanctions against the Jewish homeland.

BDS is a political agenda masquerading as a peace movement. Its literature and imagery are awash with antisemitism. BDS is not simply critical of Israeli policies; it is critical of Israel's right to exist. It vilifies the Jewish homeland to such an extent as to make reconciliation between the parties impossible. The citizens of Israel are referred to as brutal and savage; its democratic government is called a regime, and its society, apartheid and genocidal. Utterly absent in the liturgy of BDS is a call for understanding or any vision for peaceful coexistence. There is no declaration in favor of a two-state solution. In fact, there is no call from BDS for a democratic Palestinian nation that would live in peace and security with Israel.

To the contrary, many BDS groups are supported by NGOs in Europe and the US that have ties to terrorist groups. Some of the NGOs that support the BDS initiative have seemingly non-political names that would have you believe they are charities devoted to children or impoverishment in a foreign nation or an invented name that references no specific cause, recipient, or donor.[55]

There is some debate as to the origin of the economic boycott campaign. Some, such as the Lawfare Project's Brooke Goldstein,[56] trace it back to anti-Jewish boycotts before the rebirth of the Jewish homeland in 1948 and view the initial 1937 Arab boycott of Jewish products as the start of BDS. Others point to a 2001 resolution at the now infamous UN World Conference on the Elimination of Racism held in Durban, South Africa, which sought to delegitimize Israel and brand Zionism as racism.[57]

The Jew-hatred at the conference was palpable. Copies of *The Protocols of the Elders of Zion* were sold on conference grounds and anti-Israel protesters jeered participants, chanting, "Zionism is racism; Israel is apartheid" and "You have Palestinian blood on your hands." Fliers depicting Hitler with the question, "What if I had won?" circulated among conference attendees. The implied answer: "There would be NO Israel and NO Palestinian bloodshed."[58]

The academic and cultural boycott campaign clearly arrived, however, in 2004–2005 when professors and lecturers from the Palestinian Authority–controlled territories launched the Palestinian Campaign for the Academic and Cultural Boycott of Israel (PACBI) in the West Bank town of Ramallah. The organization, co-founded by Omar Barghouti and Riham Barghouti, has led global efforts to pressure international fine artists, authors, filmmakers, chefs, athletes, and musicians not to appear in Israel, claiming their presence "art washes" Israel's supposed crimes against humanity. It also pressures international venues to shun Israeli artists and athletes who receive any level of government support.

Although most of the activity is centered in Western Europe, like-minded groups can be found in dozens of countries, including Canada, the United States, South Africa, New Zealand, Hungary, and Australia.

The general campaign (all facets) is organized and coordinated by the Palestinian BDS National Committee (BNC), which operates BDSmovement.net. The website describes the BNC as a "coalition of Palestinian organisations that leads and supports the BDS movement."[59] It provides coordination, guidance, and social media messaging to international grassroots organizations and groups.[60]

Although BDS claims hundreds of such groups, it is not always possible to verify whether these organizations exist in more than name only. Oftentimes, a BDS organization will announce itself and set up pages on social media only to disappear within months or a couple of years. Membership numbers are also hard to verify.

When BDS organizations circulate petitions claiming hundreds or even tens of thousands of signatories, it is impossible to know how many of the online signatures are unique and how many are from multiple accounts belonging to the same person. Nonetheless, BDS supporters are real, and their lies and distortions are having a negative impact on the world.

Jewish Voice for Peace (JVP) is a left of center activist organization in the United States that has been active in cultural boycott campaigns against artists as well as on other fronts.[61] Adalah-NY (the New York Campaign for the Boycott of Israel) organizes numerous on-the-ground protests and is particularly active in the tristate area.[62] Independent Jewish Voices (IJV) is an active Canadian group.

The group Artists for Palestine UK (APUK) focuses on the cultural boycott of Israel. In February 2015, APUK unveiled a pledge in support of the cultural boycott that claims, as of the time of this writing, 1,350 signatories. It has produced a sixty-four-page booklet titled *The Case for a Cultural Boycott of Israel* and organizes events. Some of their better-known signatories, such as actress Miriam Margolyes, composer Brian Eno, screenwriter Paul Laverty, playwright Caryl Churchill, film director and screenwriter Michael Radford, and Scottish theater critic Mark Brown, contribute their personal comments on the organization's website. *The Guardian*, a left-of-center daily British newspaper, publishes most of its condemnatory open letters. Taking a page out of George Orwell's *1984*, APUK claims that arguments against its artistic censorship of others is censorship itself.

Although English artists such as Paul McCartney, the Rolling Stones, Elton John, Robbie Williams, Eric Clapton, Rod Stewart, Bryan Ferry, and Ozzy Osbourne continue to perform in Israel, and many have spoken out against the boycott, an organized British response to APUK has been weak.

In October 2015, just months after the release of the APUK pledge, 150 cultural workers, including J. K. Rowling, announced the creation of a new organization, Culture for Coexistence, which responded to APUK in a statement excerpted below:[63]

> We do not believe cultural boycotts are acceptable or that the letter you published accurately represents opinion in the cultural world in the UK…We will be seeking to inform and encourage dialogue about Israel and the Palestinians in the wider cultural and creative community.

The statement received international attention, and the group organized a 2017 trip to Israel with the heads of six of the UK's top art museums and galleries. As of the time of this writing, however, the website is down, and it has little traditional or social media presence.

In 2021, *Rolling Stone* magazine reported that six hundred international musicians had signed an open letter under the banner of Musicians for Palestine calling on their peers to eschew Israel.[64] Signatories include Roger Waters, Serj Tankian, Black Thought, Questlove, Thurston Moore, Julian Casablancas of The Strokes, Chromeo, Nicolas Jaar, Noname, and Owen Pallett.[65] The concept here is to have a ready-to-go statement with multiple, although mostly lesser-known, names to send to artists who book future concerts in Israel.

To understand the scope of the BDS campaign more fully, we need to briefly discuss each of its branches.

BOYCOTTS

BDS agitates for an economic, academic, and cultural embargo against Israel.

ECONOMIC BOYCOTT

The economic boycott works in tandem with the divestment campaign attempting to destabilize Israel's economy.

The economic boycott campaign wants the world to

- stop buying, selling, and promoting Israeli products;
- stop doing business with companies that do business with Israel;
- stop doing business with companies that support Israel; and

- stop buying products from Israeli companies with facilities in the disputed territories.

For example, BDS activists have called for a boycott of Brooklinen, the online sheet and linen retailer, because some of its products are made by Israel's Offis Textile. In 2020, Adalah-NY organized a small protest at Brooklinen's Williamsburg, New York, store. Two of the participants approached the staff and said they wanted to return some sheets because they were "stained with Israeli apartheid." They then pulled out pillowcases that said "Brooklinen sews destruction in Palestine" and "Brooklinen in bed with Israeli apartheid." Later, they hung the pillowcases outside the store on a clothesline.[66]

Thousands of corporations do business with Israel and dozens have headquarters there, so the potential targets for the boycott are extensive. Some of the major multinational companies that have been targeted include Caterpillar, Victoria's Secret, RE/MAX, Starbucks, Dannon Yogurt, and Nestlé.

BDS also calls for the boycott of companies that directly support Israel, or indirectly, as in the case of the Estée Lauder Companies Inc., which was boycotted due to its chairman emeritus Ronald Lauder's support for Israel. BDS has also called for a boycott of Coca-Cola because it supports the America–Israel Chamber of Commerce Awards, which honor companies that have contributed to the Israeli economy.

Although most artists who support BDS channel their energies into the cultural boycott wing, some have supported other facets of the campaign. In 2014, when Palestinians kidnapped and murdered three Israeli teenagers at a bus stop on their way home (more on that later), English actor, comic, and BDS advocate Russell Brand blamed Israel exclusively for the conflict that ensued. He taped a video urging an economic, rather than cultural, boycott of Israel, singling out Barclays bank, which he faulted for owning shares of Elbit, an Israeli high-tech security and defense company. Brand encouraged his devotees to sign a petition urging banks, pension funds, and other big businesses to sever investment ties with Israel or derail any business contracts that "facilitate the oppression of people in Gaza."[67] The petition allegedly accumulated more than 1.7 million signatories and claimed success when Barclays severed its Elbit holdings.[68]

ACADEMIC BOYCOTT

Aside from the cultural boycott campaign, the most self-destructive component of BDS must certainly be the academic wing, where education associations are working against the free exchange of ideas they claim to cherish.

Thom Yorke, lead singer of Radiohead, put it succinctly when he said, "The university thing is more of a head f*** for me. It's like, really? You can't go talk to other people who want to learn stuff in another country? Really?"[69]

Academic research requires access to information and the free exchange of ideas. Viewed as a research and development (R&D) destination of choice among US companies, Israel's academic institutions, such as the Weizmann Institute of Science, the Hebrew University of Jerusalem, and Bar-Ilan University, have made contributions in medicine, technology, and the humanities too numerous to mention here.[70] Nonetheless, there have been calls for a boycott of fine Israeli institutions from international academic associations such as the University and College Union (UCU)[71] and the American Studies Association (ASA).[72,]*

These resolutions are paradoxical given that the halls of higher learning are renowned for their progressive leanings and empathy with perceived underdogs. Former president of Al-Quds University Sari Nusseibeh noted the same, saying, "If we are to look at Israeli society, it is within the academic community that we've had the most progressive pro-peace views and views that have come out in favor of seeing us as equals. If you want to punish any sector, this is the last one to approach."[73] The academic BDS campaign, however, seeks to isolate Israeli academics regardless of their politics or position on the Israeli–Palestinian conflict.

In 2002, Harvard University president and the former treasury secretary Lawrence Summers pointed to the underlying antisemitism in the campaign, saying, "Profoundly anti-Israel views are increasingly finding support in progressive intellectual communities...Serious and thoughtful people are advocating and taking actions that are antisemitic in their effect, if not their intent."[74]

---

*   In 2018, University of Michigan professor and BDS supporter, John Chenev-Lippold, reportedly refused to write a student letter of recommendation for a study abroad program because it was in Israel. See Elizabeth Redden, "The Right to a Recommendation?" *InsideHigherEd.com*, September 19, 2018, https://www.insidehighered.com/news/2018/09/19/professor-cites-boycott-israeli-universities-declining-write-recommendation-letter; Kim Kozlowski, "UM Disciplines Prof Over Israel Letter Controversy," *The Detroit News*, October 9, 2018, https://www.detroitnews.com/story/news/local/michigan/2018/10/09/university-michigan-disciplines-professor-over-israel-letter-controversy/1580969002/.

Fortunately, many BDS resolutions fail, and some institutions, like the University of Münster, have passed anti-BDS resolutions.[75] In addition, numerous BDS initiatives have suffered academic backlash, and many administrators veto the resolutions because they violate national laws and international agreements. But the votes themselves reflect a desire to sully Israel's image and smack of antisemitism.

The academic boycott campaign on college campuses, however, mostly serves as a complement to the real damage being done inside the classrooms and on the quad. Students are being given a lopsided history lesson of the region and taught that the Israeli Jews are "white" colonists, oppressors, and racists. Palestinian violence against Jews, as well as Israel's rightful claim to the land, is ignored.

Easily debunked lies about Israel are being given false credibility when they are espoused by respected professors and intellectuals in Western universities.[76] In his book, *Industry of Lies*, author Ben-Dror Yemini does an excellent job of calling out academics such as Israeli-born Brit Ilan Pappé (arguably the father of the false charge of ethnic cleansing) and John Mearsheimer (coauthor of *The Israel Lobby*) for what he believes are their shoddy research, double standards, and politicized conclusions.[77]

Israel Apartheid Week (IAW) is a week-long, annual Israel-bashing event that descends on college campuses across the United States, Canada, and Europe in the spring. BDS groups like Students for Justice in Palestine (SJP) organize booths, pamphlets, interactive displays, and anti-Israel speakers.

Along with anti-Israel divestment resolutions, these factors have created a decidedly antizionist/antisemitic atmosphere on college campuses. Jewish and non-Jewish students who support the right of Israel to exist are excluded from positions in student government.[78] Swastikas have appeared in residence halls, and Jewish students have expressed fear for their safety.

Impressionable minds receiving misinformation about Israel can have long-term consequences. Unlearning untrue information and the beliefs and bias it creates can take a lifetime.

DIVESTMENT

The divestment campaign seeks to choke Israel financially by pressuring institutional investors, such as pension funds and school and charitable endowments, to withdraw their investments in Israeli businesses. The divestment campaign has had some successes. In 2014, the Dutch pension management fund PGGM, with assets of $200 billion, divested from five Israeli banks because of their stakes in the West Bank.[79] Fortunately, however, just five years later, in 2019, the fund removed the Israeli banks from its blacklist.[80]

The divestment campaign, however, is most visible on college campuses. Universities will often set up endowment programs where alumni and others can make charitable contributions to the school to help secure its future. These gifts are then invested in stocks, bonds, real estate, and other financial instruments to generate growth and/or income.

Anti-Israel organizations, such as Students for Justice in Palestine, work within student governments to lobby universities with resolutions to divest themselves of—or give up—their holdings in Israeli companies and companies that do business with Israel.

In addition, BDS has been smart in strategically focusing its efforts on Ivy League and other top colleges. Of the seventy-three schools that voted on BDS divestment resolutions in the last sixteen years, eleven were ranked in the top twenty, and twenty-two in the top fifty.[81] No doubt BDS proponents are aware that the students obtaining business and master's degrees at these top institutions are likely to populate the boardrooms of major corporations for years to come.

Although some students may be initially fooled, most are not. Although they garner a lot of attention, these initiatives are not as common or successful as organizations like SJP would have you think. Between 2005 and 2021, only seventy-three US campuses presented these sorts of resolutions. This represents less than 2 percent of America's 4,298 four-year colleges.[82]

Although several of the schools considered more than one resolution, 65 percent of the 147 total BDS divestment measures presented between 2005 and 2021 were defeated.[83] Furthermore, student government resolutions typically have no effect on university financial decisions. Even when students pass such resolutions, most university administrators say they have no intention of divesting from Israel. Most often, after students learn all the facts, fewer of them support the measure.

However, when you consider the initiatives in conjunction with anti-Israel indoctrination in the classroom and on the quad, there is still much to be concerned about.

SANCTIONS

International sanctions are reprimands typically occurring in multi-state organizations, such as the UN or the WHO, seeking to censure or punish a country. Sanctions can also be imposed by one country against another, as is the case with economic or trade sanctions.

A lesser form of censure is the passage of resolutions, which may state displeasure or condemnation of a nation's actions but carry no actual consequences. As a result, resolutions are more often nakedly political in nature.

For far too long, the UN, which welcomed the State of Israel into the world organization in 1949, has been the source of a disproportionate number of resolutions against the Jewish homeland. Although they are not enforceable and have no legal consequence, international condemnation underscores a poisonous anti-Israel message that can be seen as rooted in antisemitism.

In 2018, for example, the United Nations General Assembly (UNGA) adopted twenty-seven resolutions condemning different countries. One of the resolutions went against North Korea, which starves its people; one against Syria, with more than half a million slaughtered and more than a million injured; one against Iran, which exports terror; and one each against Russia, Myanmar, and the United States. All the remainder, twenty-one resolutions, were against Israel, a democratic country that guarantees free and fair elections, the rights of minorities, freedom of the press, and the rule of law.

In the six years between 2015 and 2021, UNGA approved 115 resolutions against Israel and only forty-five against the other 192 member countries combined.[84] As the New York Daily News put it, this is "even more warped considering that there are 9 million people in Israel out of 7.9 billion on Earth. So, Israelis are 0.1% of the world, but they still get almost three-fourth of the UN's brickbats."[85]

The UN Human Rights Council (UNHRC), which has allowed terrorist states such as Iran as members but denied membership to Israel, demonstrates the same outrageous bias. According to UNWatch.org, from its creation in June 2006 through June 2016, the UNHRC adopted 135 resolutions criticizing countries; sixty-eight out of those 135 resolutions (more than 50 percent) have been against Israel.[86]

In 2020, the UN published a database of more than one hundred companies it says are doing business in the Palestinian territories. It spent more than three years compiling this blacklist, which BDS leaders gratefully acknowledged would help their "cause."[87]

So, why is Israel, the only Jewish state on the planet, the one country to be consistently singled out for condemnation by the international community when countries that export terrorism and slaughter their citizens are practically ignored? The answer lies in the composition of the governing body.

The UNGA is one of the six main bodies of the UN and the main deliberative and policy-making organ of the organization. It is the only UN body in which all member states have equal representation: one nation, one vote. The Organization of Islamic Cooperation (OIC) represents fifty-six of the 193 member states in the UNGA, nearly 30 percent of the votes necessary to pass a resolution.[88] The OIC is a consistent source of resolutions and votes against Israel.

Although the UN resolutions against Israel are biased and ill-intended, BDS proponents use them as evidence to justify their campaign.

BDS HYPOCRISY

Although BDS and its supporters talk a big game about boycotting Israeli companies and academics, they are avid consumers of Israeli technology and innovation.

Like everyone else in the world, they use Israeli technology such as online chat, Voice over Internet Protocol (VoIP), USB flash drives, Waze, Wix software for website design, Intel processors, solar water heaters, and drip irrigation for agriculture. The campaign has no qualms about allowing its followers to use medical cures that come out of Israel[89] but calls for a boycott of the means (including academic exchange) that enable the country to discover them.

Although BDS leadership claims that its campaign is a Palestinian civil society effort, PACBI co-founder Omar Barghouti is not exactly a native son. Barghouti was born in Qatar and is of Palestinian descent. He grew up in Egypt, married a Palestinian Israeli, and moved to Israel as an adult. Barghouti did not choose to support the boycott himself by continuing his studies in Qatar or Egypt or attending any one of the eleven universities in the West Bank or the seven universities in Gaza (almost all of which were established after the Israeli takeover of the territories in 1967).[90] Instead, he holds a master's degree in electrical engineering from Columbia University and earned a master's degree in philosophy and is working on a PhD from Tel Aviv University.[91] Apparently, the Qatari/Egyptian/Palestinian Barghouti advocates against academic exchange with Israel except when it comes to his own education—then he wants the best there is.

Many people have been hoodwinked into thinking the objective of the BDS campaign is to simply create a new, independent Palestinian state, free of the so-called "occupation." Not so according to Barghouti, who rejects the two-state solution and the very idea of a Jewish state anywhere in the original Palestinian Mandate. "No Palestinian, rational Palestinian, not a sell-out Palestinian," according to Baghouti, "will ever accept a Jewish state in Palestine."[92] For the co-founder of the BDS campaign, there are no dual claims or "both sides" to this debate. He argues that the Palestinians have inalienable rights, while Jewish rights are at best "acquired" rights, even if they receive international recognition.

Furthermore, he maintains that the establishment of an independent Palestinian state would not end the call for boycotts, divestments, and sanctions against Israel. "If the occupation ends, let's say, would that end your call for BDS? No, it wouldn't," he asks and then answers.[93] For Barghouti, the key element of the movement is the "right" of all Palestinian refugees, from all over the world, to return to Israel and become citizens (the "Right of Return"). This, according to Barghouti, is "the most fundamental, basic right that we cannot negotiate away...This is something that we cannot compromise on."[94] Why? Because, says Barghouti, "If the refugees were to return, you will not have a two-state solution... 'You will have a Palestine next to a Palestine...'"[95]

And for me, as well as President Barack Obama, "That is not an option."[96]

* * *

The ship has pretty much sailed on the current educational system in the United States. Israel's enemies have spent decades and hundreds of millions, if not billions, of dollars institutionalizing Jew-hatred into our education curriculum. We have all but lost a generation.

Should we continue to sign statements, write our congressional representatives, and attend rallies in protest? Yes, we should. We should not tolerate Jew-hatred, wherever it appears. However, it will take a Herculean effort to reverse the systemic antizionism in our education institutions and at the UN. And the best way to break the formidable Arab-nation, anti-Israel voting bloc in the UN is the formation of more peace treaties between Israel and these countries, not criticism from the world citizenry.

The cultural boycott campaign against Israel, however, is a different story. It relies on social and mainstream media to disseminate antizionist lies and pressure international artists and venues to discriminate against Israeli audiences and artists. These weapons are available to the rest of us as well, and we must use them and take up the fight.

In the past, when violence against Jews has descended into the streets—as it has now in Los Angeles, New York City, Toronto, and London—we have taken mezuzahs off our doorposts, kippahs off our heads, and Jewish stars off our necks.

We do not have to do that anymore. We can fight back. It is time to demand the end to Jew-hatred and insist on consequences for people who inflame it.

NEXT STEP: ENGAGE.

Add your voice to the conversation.

Retweet and like my posts, even if you do not want to comment.

If you are not on social media and do not want to be, do you know someone who is? Send them a copy of this book and see if they are inspired to get engaged.

CHAPTER SIX

LIFTING THE VEIL

"I believe strongly that cultural dialogue and collaboration is more important than ever before and that cultural boycotts are divisive, discriminatory and counter-productive."

—J. K. ROWLING, BRITISH AUTHOR

Proponents of the cultural Boycott, Divestment, and Sanctions campaign against Israel claim their cause is human rights and their methods are nonviolent. They have mastered the language of the enlightened left, but scratch the surface and you will see that their tactics—along with their messaging—are anything but peaceful.

Most international entertainers who want to perform in Israel face threats to their careers, their reputations, and even their lives from the cultural boycott organizations and their supporters.

INTIMIDATION

One of the key differences between the cultural boycott of Israel and the rest of the BDS movement is the laser focus on an individual.

Artists make easy targets. Statements and graphics associating the artist with racism, war, and destruction are seen by tens of thousands, if not hundreds of thousands, of people. The threat to the artist's career is obvious. Who wants to attend the concert of a racist? And in case the threat to the artist's livelihood is not clear enough, individual zealots typically post comments on Facebook and Twitter that directly attack how these performers earn their livings, such as, "I used to buy all your music, but now…"

Managers for Salif Keita, an albino Afropop singer-songwriter, canceled his scheduled tour in Israel for fear of both personal and professional harm. Posting on Facebook, his management said BDS groups "threatened…to work diligently at ruining the reputation and career that Mr. Keita has worked 40 years to achieve."[97]

BDS does not seek to educate; it seeks to intimidate. Associating artists with violence leads to violent threats against artists. Before his concert in Tel Aviv, Paul McCartney was warned by Islamic activist Omar Bakri Muhammad, "If he values his life Mr. McCartney must not come to Israel. He will not be safe there."[98]

Singer Eric Burdon, formerly of the Animals, canceled a scheduled performance in northern Israel with the Israeli band Tislam. "We are under increasing pressure, including many threatening emails that we are receiving on a daily basis. I wouldn't want to put Eric in any danger," Burdon's representative wrote to the band.[99] Burdon would later recommit to the performance, telling *Yisrael Hayom*, "It wasn't my decision to cancel the show, but that of my manager, following numerous threatening emails, she was scared for my life."[100]

A concert promoter I know told me that the lead singer of a heavy metal band canceled a performance after being barraged, saying, "I won't risk my life in order to perform in Israel."

The undeniable fact is that the cultural boycott campaign threatens artists. It does so purposefully, threatening their careers and their good names, and whether it is intended or not, the heightened vitriol also leads to fears about their physical safety.

Could BDS demonization of artists lead to violent acts against artists by BDS supporters or others? I certainly hope not, but in my opinion, it is extremely dangerous. As film historian and documentary filmmaker James Forsher noted in connection with warfare propaganda, "The secret in propaganda is that when you demonize, you dehumanize. When you dehumanize, it allows you to kill your enemy and no longer feel guilty about it."[101]

CENSORSHIP

In 2016, I attended a conference at the University of California, Irvine, titled "Freedom of Expression in a Changing World: What Cannot Be Said." A key point made by several speakers, including Nicholas Goldberg, then-editor of the editorial pages at the *Los Angeles Times*, was that censorship in contemporary Western societies is not coming from governments in the form of laws and police crackdowns; it is coming from segments of the politically motivated public. Nowhere is that censorship more evident than in the cultural boycott campaign against Israel, which effects both international and Israeli artists.

There are two essential ingredients necessary for freedom of artistic expression to thrive: the freedom to create and the freedom to share. That is true for every artist, regardless of his or her medium. Art is a shared experience. Artists want to take their personal experiences, thoughts, and emotions and put them in a form that resonates in the hearts and minds of another human being, hopefully millions of human beings, hopefully over many, many years.

The cultural boycott effort seeks to control both the content and distribution of art. Do you know where else we see that? In totalitarian regimes. Totalitarian regimes burn books, cut off the means of communication, and jail performers. By suppressing the distribution and consumption of art and creating litmus tests for artists, BDS tactics are only mildly less dangerous.

In the summer of 2015, a Spanish music festival initially succumbed to boycott pressure from BDS proponents and canceled a performance by Jewish American reggae singer Matisyahu. Why? Because he refused to comply with BDS demands to produce a personal statement in alignment with their position on the Israeli–Palestinian conflict. The festival subsequently reissued an invitation but only following a condemnation by Spanish authorities and the United States embassy in Madrid.

According to a report by the *Times of Israel*, the organizers blamed the local anti-Israel group BDS País Valencià, which campaigned to cancel Matisyahu's invitation, for alleged "pressures, threats and coercion," efforts that seemed poised to "seriously disrupt the normal functioning of the festival" and "prevented the management of the situation with clarity."[102]

It is not just artists and Israelis who suffer at the hands of the cultural boycott, but art lovers. BDS disregards the ideal that it is the individual, not a politically motivated third party, who should decide what he or she wishes to experience.

The threat to freedom of expression anywhere is a threat to that freedom everywhere. BDS is creating a handbook for the repression of artistic expression in democratic societies. The world looks away at great peril.

OPPOSITION TO CULTURAL EXCHANGE

Utterly absent in BDS rhetoric is a call for artists to foster peace and reconciliation. Artists are routinely shunned for their attempts to bring both sides together or for expressing any sign of a balanced perspective.

The cultural boycott campaign is adamantly opposed to any sort of cultural exchange or bridging of differences through the arts. It routinely rejects offers by artists who want to play for audiences in both Tel Aviv and the Palestinian territories. To supporters of the cultural boycott, it is not enough for artists to care about the Palestinian people; they must unequivocally renounce Israel.

In March 2017, British comedian, actor, and writer Eddie Izzard was banned from running in a Palestinian marathon that organizers claimed was raising awareness about the restrictions on freedom of movement for Palestinians. The opposition came from the event organizers, PACBI, and APUK.

Izzard is well known for outspokenness, brilliant comic monologues, and gender fluidity.* It was not Izzard's personal life, however, that made her persona non grata; her sin was performing a comedy concert in Israel the day before the marathon. "British comedian Eddie Izzard cannot run for freedom this Friday if he [sic] entertains in Tel Aviv on Thursday," the official Twitter account of the marathon stated. "We refuse to be used as a fig leaf to cover up Izzard's whitewashing of Israel's occupation and apartheid."[103]

In 2016, the socially conscious comedian ran twenty-seven marathons as a tribute to Nelson Mandela's twenty-seven years in prison during South Africa's apartheid regime. The Palestinian "freedom" marathon route passed through Bethlehem and several refugee camps and alongside Israel's security barrier. Undoubtedly, Izzard's involvement would have shined additional light on some of the challenges Palestinians face, if that were what the boycott leaders cared about, but it seems it was not.

The Brit backed out gracefully, saying, "All I wanted to do was to try and bring a little extra focus to the Palestine Marathon and to the situation there. But if they would rather I didn't, I'm fine with that. But good luck to all the runners and I hope they run great marathons."[104]

---

* Izzard announced the preferred use of she/her/hers for pronouns in 2019. Jenny Mensah, "Eddie Izzard Doesn't Mind if You Get Her Pronouns Wrong," RadioX, January 13, 2021, https://www.radiox.co.uk/news/tv-film/eddie-izzard-doesnt-mind-pronouns-wrong/#:~:text=The%20British%20comedian%2C%20actor%20and,%2C%20our%20continent%2C%20our%20world.

Once again, Palestinians get the short end of the stick as BDS seemingly prefers demonizing Israel over progress for the people.

IMPACT ON ARTISTS

What is often ignored about the cultural boycott campaign is the impact it has on the artists themselves. Success does not make artists immune to the sting of attempted character assassination. These assaults on their reputations are played out on the world stage and linger forever in cyberspace. Entertainers, authors, actors, filmmakers, and especially musicians are vulnerable when ambushed.

Sometimes, people will make the irrelevant and unfounded argument that the artists targeted by BDS do not really care how they are talked about—they are just playing in Israel for the money.

Artists play in Israel for the same reason they play everywhere else. Of course, they want to be compensated for their work, but they also want to connect with their fans. They want to realize their unique ability to challenge us, make us think, bring us together, create universality, and provide a bedrock for peace.

Success is not an anesthetic. It does not make one immune to the pain and public humiliation of public rebut. The bigger the artist, the bigger the media storm, and the more widespread the false accusations.

In addition, although conversation often focuses on high-profile celebrities, it is the lesser-known artists who can end up bearing the brunt of the BDS effort. Tour dates and sales mean a great deal to them and their families. Threats to their careers, implied or explicit, strike home, and BDS callously exploits this vulnerability.

Martha Wainwright is the sister of musician Rufus Wainwright and a talented folk-rock singer-songwriter. In 2014, she ignored inflammatory boycott calls and performed for her fans in Israel.

The next stop on her multi-country tour was at the Trades Club in West Yorkshire, England, a socialist member coopera-tive, club, bar, and music venue. In seeming retaliation for her performance in Israel, BDS demanded the club withdraw the invitation and threatened a picket. The club reluctantly kept Wainwright's date because they were contractually obligat-ed.[105] An official statement, however, made no bones about the chances of her future employment, saying in part, "In common with many others, the Trades Club is very disappointed to dis-cover that Martha Wainwright recently chose to play in Israel. The Club had no prior knowledge of her intention to do so when we made the booking. We support the cultural boycott of Israel and would not knowingly engage anyone who has or intends to contravene it."[106]

The night of her performance, Wainwright broke down in tears after being heckled by the audience. The Facebook page "Martha Wainwright, Everything Wrong with Israeli Apartheid" is still active as of June 2021, with more than 1,300 likes.[107]

BDS attempts to create a "chilling effect" whereby artists will decline to perform in Israel in the first place to avoid the unwar-ranted smear on their names. Is that sometimes effective? Yes, it is. In a confidential conversation with one of Israel's most successful concert promoters, I was told artists occasionally say they would love to perform in Israel, but "it's just not worth it." According to promoter Daniel Ben Av, Ed Sheeran declined an invitation to do a concert in Tel Aviv with a similar sentiment. Although BDS may rejoice in that result, it is crucial for all to remember the chilling effect it works so hard to achieve is in fact a form of censorship.

Whether an artist censors himself or herself out of fear of public reprisal or as a direct result of government restrictions, the result is the same. The subtlety of self-censorship might be lost on the public, but it is of utmost concern to the artist community.

If you think BDS is a nonviolent campaign with humanistic goals, think again.

NEXT STEP: REMEMBER, ARTISTS ARE VICTIMS AS WELL.

Artists do not like cultural boycotts. When they are attacked by BDS, engage them on social media and give them a reason to keep their concert dates.

Underscore their role as agents of peace.

Ask artists to go to Israel to learn about it for themselves. Unlike BDS, Israel has nothing to hide.

Ask them to help us put an end to Jew-hatred.

CHAPTER SEVEN

THE PROGRESSIVE LEFT

"The world view of Israel is just not reality."

—LADY GAGA, AMERICAN SINGER-SONGWRITER

So, if BDS is bad for artists, why would any of them support it?

Although artists may lead what appear to us as extraordinary lives, they get their information the same way the rest of us do—through mainstream news and social media. They have been fed BDS lies about Israel by universities. When artists visit Israel, they learn the truth for themselves—Israel is a diverse society with a vibrant democracy—which, in my view, is one reason why BDS does not want them to go there. The propaganda and manipulative imagery that BDS feeds the American and world citizenry are contrary to the reality on the ground.

Many BDS advocates and "Israel Bashers" (those who bash Israel while falling short of a call to boycott) join the cause because of their progressive politics. The progressive social concept of "intersectionality" has created a false symmetry between the Palestinians and people of color in the West and a correlating anti-Israel bias.

"Intersectionality" is a modern sociological term coined in 1989 by Kimberlé Crenshaw,[108] a civil rights activist and law professor, that is often heard but less often understood. Initially, the concept referred to the idea that Black women are the victims of both racism and sexism, and this overlap, or intersect, increases the discrimination they face.

The term has since morphed and typically refers to the common interests of many kinds of oppressed groups. In 2015, the *Oxford English Dictionary* defined it as "the interconnected nature of social categorizations such as race, class, and gender, regarded as creating overlapping and interdependent systems of discrimination or disadvantage."[109]

A key word in this definition is "interdependent" (i.e., depending on one another). This has led to the idea that oppressed groups should support one another because their interests—fighting oppression—"intersect."

The construct, however, leaves Jews, as an ethnic group, out. Why? Because despite all the centuries of discrimination, expulsions, and mass murder, Jews are not considered to be disadvantaged or oppressed and therefore are not believed to need protection. Unlike other minorities in the West, as previously discussed, Jews are associated with wealth and power. And therefore, as David Baddiel puts it, they are being "left out, by the left, of identity politics."[110]

To be clear, this exclusion does not apply to individual Jews who are also the victims of other sources of oppression. Gay Jews are welcome. So are non-white Jews. They are welcomed into "the sacred circle of the oppressed,"[111] to borrow a phrase coined by Baddiel, because they are gay or brown and despite, not because, they are Jewish.

And even though the majority of Jews in Israel are people of color descending from North Africa and the Middle East (and whose ancestors did not reside in Europe) and all Jews are indigenous to the land of Israel, Israeli Jews have been reimagined as white colonizers and the enemies of progressive activism.

BDS has capitalized on the social justice movements of the West and disguises itself as a pro-peace, human-rights movement. It appeals to Western guilt about European colonization, a sin for which Israel bears no responsibility. Unlike the colonists from England, Holland, France, Belgium, and Spain, Jews were refugees fleeing persecution, not representatives of a mother country. They did not steal the riches of a foreign soil; they purchased the land and turned a desert into an oasis in their ancestral home.

BDS conflates itself with established progressive movements but denigrates the most liberal and democratic country in the Middle East and fosters anti-Jewish hate. It cynically uses the language of the left and talks about freedom, justice, and equality, but, as Jeremy Ben-Ami, president of J Street, has noted, it:[112]

> doesn't acknowledge the right of the Jewish people to be free in their own land. It recognizes the right of self-determination of

the Palestinian people but not of the Jewish people…You have a whole influx of support for the BDS movement from well-meaning liberals, who don't really understand what was the BDS charter, and what are the fundamental principles on which it was founded.

BDS does not have a plan for peaceful coexistence with Israel or prosperity for the Palestinian population. The "plan" starts and ends with getting rid of the Jews.

Artists are as blind and numb to systemic Jew-hatred as everyone else. When they repeat BDS falsehoods about "stolen Palestinian land," for example, they are blind to the "greedy, thieving Jews" trope buried within that accusation.

Artists all over the world tend to lean left. In one of my many conversations with actor Mark Pellegrino, I asked him to share his thoughts on that and particularly why so many artists and others on the left are willing to compartmentalize their other values to condemn Israel. Pellegrino noted that the arts rely heavily on the expression of emotion, and BDS speaks in emotionally manipulative sound bites to tell its story. Accordingly, he feels that BDS harps on the false charges of apartheid and the murder of children because that gets people feeling instead of thinking, and he told me that Israel's position requires "a narrative and abstract thought."

This conservative/progressive alignment regarding Israel is terribly misplaced. I support Israel not despite some of my left-of-center values but because of them. Israel has been a leader in LGBTQ+ and women's rights, water conservation and desalination, reforestation, sustainable non-fossil energy, the fight against global warming, and socialized medicine. It is disturbing to me that most of Israel's progressive policies are either ignored or given scant acknowledgment by the left-leaning West. Like many others from both US political parties, I believe in a just resolution to the conflict with the Palestinians resulting in two states—an independent Palestinian state and a Jewish Israeli state—living side by side in peace and security.

As you will see throughout this book, some politically progressive artists have used their platforms to disseminate hyperbolic and antisemitic disinformation about Israel. We must ask artists and others to understand what they are saying and the potential tragedy that can come from their words. When they do not fully educate themselves about the history of the Jews and the region (meaning both Palestinian *and* Israeli narratives), their opinions most often end up doing more harm than good.

NEXT STEP: GET ON SOCIAL MEDIA.

Many people, like me, do not particularly like social media. However, this is where public opinion is being made.

Pick one forum and have someone teach you how to use it if you do not already know. You do not even have to post or comment to make a difference. Just liking and sharing the posts of others will help.

We cannot allow Israel-haters to monopolize the conversation. They are rewriting history to determine the future.

CHAPTER EIGHT

THE HISTORY OF THE REGION

*"The Jews have lived in Israel for 4000
years. They are indigenous peoples."*

—DEBRA MESSING, AMERICAN ACTRESS

Israel is not perfect; it makes mistakes. But it is not racist, genocidal, or apartheid. My love for Israel is an integral part of my
Jewishness and a source of pride for me, as it is for millions of
other Jews across the globe. Sadly, Israel's supporters frequently
get attacked and incorrectly feel like they need to be experts
on all things Israel to defend it. It is not important, however,
that you are deeply knowledgeable about every bit of history
or savvy regarding each current event. It is important only that
you understand and feel our rightful place on this land.

Here are a few key points to keep in mind:

- Jews are indigenous to the land of Israel.
- The modern State of Israel was established by legal means.

- There is not now, nor has there ever been, a sovereign Arab state called Palestine.
- Israel is a democracy that guarantees equal treatment under the law to all its citizens.

The Jewish people have had a connection to the land of Israel since King David established sovereignty there more than three thousand years ago. The borders of the kingdom changed throughout the centuries due to wars and internal conflicts. At times, it stretched far north and south of today's boundaries and east of the Jordan River into modern-day Jordan. In the tenth century, it divided into two kingdoms, Israel in the north and Judea in the south (Jews get their name from Judea). Today, the region known as Judea and Samaria most commonly refers to the disputed territory west of the Jordan River, which many Palestinians want as a future state, but is also used by some to describe the entire ancient homeland of the Jewish people.

The Romans conquered the land in the first century CE and renamed it Palestine in the second century (after the Philistines, an Aegean people, who were not Arab or Muslim). Although over the following centuries the territory was conquered by numerous foreign powers, forcing Jews into exile (the Diaspora), Jews have always maintained a presence there, and the longing to return to Jerusalem has been a mainstay in Jewish liturgy.[113]

Zionism is both an ideology of Jewish liberation and a nationalist movement that espouses the establishment of, and support for, a Jewish state. It was founded in 1896 by Theodor Herzl[114] in response to the centuries of violence and discrimination against Jews in the diaspora. At that time, the region was under Turkish rule, and the Arabs, Jews, and other people living there were citizens of the Ottoman (Turkish) Empire. Jewish organizations and individual Jews purchased land at fair market value, mostly in areas that were sparsely populated or where the local Arabs were tenants, not landowners.[115] Much of the future farmland was swamp, and hundreds of early Jewish pioneers lost their lives to malaria.

At the end of World War I, the Allied Powers dismantled the Ottoman Empire, which had sided with Germany during the war. In 1920, the League of Nations, which was the predecessor of the UN, granted the French control of Mandate Syria and Lebanon. The English got control over Iraq and Palestine, the latter of which was referred to as the "British Mandate" or "Palestine Mandate." This area included the territories that are today Jordan, the West Bank, and Israel.

The purpose of the British Mandate was to oversee the founding of a new Jewish state on that land, but the Jews were not the only people benefiting from this nation-building in the post–World War I era. As Israeli actress, producer, and author Noa Tishby notes in her book, *Israel—A Simple Guide to the Most Misunderstood Country on Earth*, "The prenationalistic, prewar Middle East was not divided into counties or borders as we understand them today. It was an ancient web of tribal affiliations, religions, and ethnic groups that operated in a huge open region, controlled mostly by the Ottomans."[116] Their connections and obligations were decentralized mainly to families, towns, and districts.[117]

Many of the Arab nations that we recognize today as independent countries, such as Iraq (1932), Saudi Arabia (1932), Lebanon (1946), Syria (1946), and Jordan (1946), did not exist before the end of the First World War.

As documented in the *Encyclopaedia Britannica*:[118]

> The idea that Palestinians form a distinct people is relatively recent.
> The Arabs living in Palestine had never had a separate state. Until
> the establishment of Israel, the term Palestinian was used by Jews
> and foreigners to describe the inhabitants of Palestine and had
> only begun to be used by the Arabs themselves at the turn of the
> 20th century. With the Arab world in a period of renaissance
> popularizing notions of Arab unity and nationalism amid the
> decline of the Ottoman Empire, most saw themselves as part of
> the larger Arab or Muslim community.

The idea of Palestinian nationhood only gained traction after
the 1967 war, in large part due to the efforts of the Palestine
Liberation Organization (PLO) led by Yasser Arafat.

In 1921, Winston Churchill severed three-fourths of the land
from the Palestine Mandate and earmarked it for Transjordan
(a.k.a. Jordan), creating yet another Arab state and drastically
reducing the size of the future Jewish homeland.

In 1922, the League of Nations officially approved the establishment of a Jewish national home in Palestine (in the reduced
area) and the preservation of the civil and religious, but not
the political or national, rights of the non-Jewish Palestinian
communities.[119]

The Arabs in the area disapproved of the resolution and began
attacking and killing their Jewish neighbors. By the mid-1930s,
their dissatisfaction had grown into open rebellion.[120]

The Peel Commission, headed by Lord Robert Peel, was

appointed in 1936 by the British government to investigate the causes of unrest among Palestinian Arabs and Jews. The report asserted the mandate was unworkable because Jewish and Arab objectives in Palestine were incompatible, and it proposed the remaining Palestinian land be partitioned into three zones: an Arab state, a Jewish state, and a neutral territory containing Jerusalem's Holy Places.[121]

In 1947, following the Peel Commission recommendation, the UN Partition Plan was approved to recognize a Jewish state and an Arab state in the remaining area of the Palestine Mandate, with Jerusalem governed separately by an international administration. Although the territory was a much smaller area than what they had been promised and noncontiguous, the Jews embraced their new home and declared independence on May 14, 1948. Almost a year later, on May 11, 1949, Israel was admitted into the UN.

The Arabs in the region, however, did not accept the 1947 partition plan, and an independent Palestinian Arab state was never established.

Instead, in 1948, the local Arab population, along with Arabs in Lebanon, Syria, Iraq, and Egypt (Saudi Arabia sent a formation that fought under the Egyptian command), went to war against the nascent Jewish state.*

At the end of the 1948 war, known as the War of Independence, the map in the area changed. Israel expanded so that it was now contiguous, while Jordan occupied and later annexed East Jeru-

---

* The antagonism has never been solely a Palestinian–Israeli conflict; it has always been an Arab-Israeli conflict.

salem (including the Old City and its Holy Places) as well as the West Bank, and Egypt occupied the Gaza Strip (the local Arabs did not demand a separate state for themselves in the West Bank and Gaza, although they could have under the partition plan). The Israelis gained control over West Jerusalem, the Galilee, and the bigger parts of the Negev desert. The Jewish homeland, however, was still only nine miles wide at its narrowest point, leaving it vulnerable to enemy attack.

The so-called "Green Line" is the armistice, or ceasefire, line set out in the 1949 Armistice Agreements between the armies of Israel and those of its neighbors (Egypt, Jordan, Lebanon, and Syria) after the 1948 war.[122] It was intended to create a stasis, or a period of inactivity, while an attempt was made to negotiate a lasting peace. The name comes from the green ink used to draw the line on the map while the armistice talks were going on.

Over the next nineteen years, Jordan barred Jews from the Old City and denied them access to the Western Wall and other Holy Places. The Jewish Quarter in the Old City was destroyed; fifty-eight synagogues were desecrated. Thousands of tombstones in the Jewish cemetery on the Mount of Olives were pulled up and used to pave roads and build fences and latrines in Jordanian army camps.[123] Palestinians launched hundreds of attacks against the Israeli civilian population from both the Gaza Strip and the West Bank.

The War of Independence also rendered a shift in populations and, as most wars do, created refugees. Approximately 750,000 Jews were forced out of or left their homes in the neighboring Arab nations and immigrated to Israel as refugees. Approximately the same number of Arabs were forced out of or left their homes in Israel and also became refugees. During the war, the Arab nations encouraged the local Arabs to leave, promising them a swift and glorious return to their homes after Israel was defeated. Some of the Arab refugees were the descendants of families that had been living in the region for generations; others were not. To qualify as a Palestinian refugee, one only had to establish that one had been living in Palestine for at least two years.

The Jews were absorbed by the Jewish state and became citizens. The members of the Arab population who did not flee also became Israeli citizens, although some refused citizenship. Arab Israelis have more rights and freedoms than Arabs living in any other part of the Middle East.

Many of the Arab refugees who fled to other Arab countries were not integrated into the populations and were placed into refugee camps with very few rights. However, unlike any other refugee population in the world, the descendants of those original Palestinian refugees are considered refugees regardless of where they live or whether they are citizens of other countries. So, for example, although most of the two million Palestinian refugees in Jordan have been granted Jordanian citizenship, they are still registered as refugees by UN Relief and Works Agency for Palestine Refugees (UNWRA).[124] Thus, instead of shrinking over the last seventy-plus years, the number of official Palestinian refugees has swelled. As of 2019, approximately 5.6 million Palestinians were registered as refugees with UNRWA.[125] The Palestinians are the only people whose refugee status is inheritable.

In June 1967, Israel was threatened by encroaching Arab troops and fought and defeated the combined armies of Egypt, Syria, and Jordan. The map changed yet again when Israel captured the West Bank, East Jerusalem, the Gaza Strip, the Golan Heights, and the Sinai Peninsula in what is known as the Six-Day War. Jordan abandoned its interest and authority in the West Bank, and Israel assumed its administration.*

Soon thereafter, Israel was willing to negotiate land for peace, but the Arabs felt humiliated and refused. In August and September 1967, eight Arab heads of state attended the Arab League summit, which was convened in Khartoum, the capital of Sudan, and issued a resolution that called for the continued struggle against Israel. The so-called Khartoum Resolution is famous for containing what became known as "The Three Nos": no peace with Israel, no recognition of Israel, and no negotiations with Israel.[126] The Arabs once again missed an opportunity to create an independent Palestinian country.

Although the territories captured by Israel beyond the Green Line in 1967 are often referred to as Israeli-occupied territories, they are in fact "disputed" lands, and Israel has a legitimate claim to them. (More on that later.)

Around the early 1970s, Israelis began building Jewish com-

---

* Multiple generations of Afghan, Bhutanese, Burmese, Nepalese, Thai, Tibetan, and Somali people have been recognized as refugees under UNHCR but only if the multiple generations all fit the primary 1951 definition of a refugee (i.e., a person who "owing to well-founded fear of being persecuted for reasons of race, religion, nationality, membership of a particular social group or political opinion, is outside the country of his nationality and is unable or, owing to such fear, is unwilling to avail himself of the protection of that country"), not simply because they are the descendants of the original male refugee. Furthermore, it is worth noting that every other refugee around the world is aided and protected by UNHRC. Palestinian refugees are the only refugees who have an agency devoted to them—UNWRA—and as the number of Palestinians has swelled, so has UNWRA's budget.

munities in the West Bank, Gaza, and the Sinai Peninsula. Palestinian Arabs were and continue to be resistant to and angered by this development. However, the idea that these settlements are (or *were* in the case of Gaza and Sinai)† illegal derives primarily from UN resolutions and the International Court of Justice (ICJ), which is an arm of the UN, and is arguably a result of the UN's previously discussed anti-Israel bias.[127]

In 1993, talks between the Israelis and Palestinians led to the Oslo Accords, which included clear criteria for progress toward Palestinian independence and the establishment of the Palestinian Authority (PA).[128] The interim agreement provided for self-government and the election of a Palestinian council but also required that the PA rein in terrorism as a precondition to any political progress,[129] which it has steadfastly failed to do. Nonetheless, today, Hamas governs Gaza, and the PA governs the parts of the West Bank where the Palestinian Arabs are the most populous.

In the Camp David–Taba negotiations of 2000–2001, Israeli prime minister Barak offered the Palestinians a state with its capital in Jerusalem, a return of approximately 97 percent of the West Bank and all the Gaza Strip, sovereignty over Arab neighborhoods of Jerusalem, and a $30 billion compensation package for refugees.[130] Yasser Arafat, however, rejected this historic offer and shortly thereafter launched the terrorism spree known as the Second Intifada against Israeli citizens. Suicide bombers murdered innocent Israeli civilians in pizza parlors and children on buses.

---

† In 1979, Israel returned the Sinai to Egypt as part of a peace treaty and in 2005 withdrew from the Gaza Strip.

In 2005, Israel unilaterally withdrew entirely from the Gaza Strip, uprooting Jewish residents and Jewish remains in cemeteries to forge a unilateral peace and leaving behind thousands of greenhouses. Instead of reciprocating with gestures of peace or improving the lives of the residents, Palestinian militants in Gaza destroyed the greenhouses and launched thousands of rocket and mortar attacks at Israeli citizens that continue to this day.

In 2006, the citizens of Gaza elected Hamas, a terrorist organization devoted to the destruction of Israel, as their leadership. The Hamas Party and the PA were instantly at each other's throats, and Gaza descended into violence with each side accusing the other of executions and tossing members of the opposing party from rooftops to their deaths.[131] The chronic dissension between the two factions has left Israel with no clear negotiating partner.

Israel has, however, reached agreements with willing partners. In 1979, Egyptian president Anwar al-Sadat and Israeli prime minister Menachem Begin negotiated a peace agreement that restored Egyptian sovereignty in the Sinai and has continued to last to this day. In 1994, Israel signed a peace agreement with Jordan. The 2021 Abraham Accords established diplomatic relations and full normalization between Israel and the United Arab Emirates, Bahrain, Sudan, and Morocco.

There is so much misinformation and disagreement about what is commonly referred to as "Palestine" and the Palestinian people that it is difficult to untangle it all, and it is not the aim of this book to do so. It does bear noting, however, that what constitutes "Palestinian lands" varies depending on who is speaking. To some, it is the disputed territory of the West Bank and (sometimes) Gaza. To others, it is all the territory beyond the Green Line except the Sinai (i.e., the Golan Heights, East Jerusalem, the West Bank, and Gaza). To others still (including the BDS leadership and enthusiasts), it is all the above plus Israel. When protesters chant, "From the river to the sea, Palestine will be free," they are calling for the extinction of Israel (no Israel anywhere between the Jordan River and the Mediterranean Sea).

The biggest misconception, however, is that Palestine is presently an independent Arab state; it is not. That does not mean, however, that it cannot or should not become one—if Israel is both recognized as a Jewish state by its neighbor and guaranteed security.

Today, Arabs living in the West Bank and Gaza clearly identify as Palestinian, but so do some Arab citizens of Israel. Large numbers of the original refugees and descendants of the original refugees self-identify as hyphenates of the countries in which they are now citizens (e.g., Palestinian-American). In this book, the term "Palestinian" is used to refer to the non-Jewish residents of Gaza and the West Bank, and the terms "Palestinian Israelis" and "Arab Israelis" refer to citizens of the State of Israel who are of Palestinian descent.

Israel is a country where all citizens are equal under the law regardless of their race, religion, gender, or sexual orientation. Since its founding, Arab Israelis have held positions in government and have been members of the Israeli judiciary. Israel is a multicultural, diverse population of all hues made up of citizens whose heritage obtains as much or more from African and Arab countries as from European and Soviet. It is a place of refuge for every Jew fleeing antisemitism, religious persecution, and ethnic bigotry. It is a "homecoming" for all Jews who dream of living their lives in their ancestral homeland.

Nowadays, the world is sensitized to the damage that words can do. We are careful about the way we speak about people of color, LGBTQ+ people, immigrants, and women and respect their histories of oppression. What about the most victimized ethnic group in the world? Don't we warrant the same consideration?

It is usually not hard for politically conservative people to criticize the thinking of the progressive left on Israel or any other matter, and vice-versa. However, the right of self-determination for the Jews is not a left/right issue; it is a human rights issue. Therefore, it is critical that all people of conscience denounce antisemitism in all its forms regardless of which side of the aisle it is coming from.

NEXT STEP: APPEAL VS. ATTACK.

Point out that people are not even aware of the antisemitism that is inside of them because it is so systemic and intergenerational.

Ask them to reflect on their biases. They might think that their disparaging remarks about Israeli Jews somehow do not count. Let them know—they do.

Tell your progressive friends that being an anti-racist means being against Jew-hatred and calling out antisemitism.

CHAPTER NINE

THE MAN BEHIND THE CURTAIN

*"What is with Roger Waters and the Jews? Where do you want the Jews to go, Roger? You want them just to go back to the concentration camps? What is it you want, f*ckhead?"*

—HOWARD STERN, AMERICAN RADIO AND
TELEVISION PERSONALITY AND AUTHOR

In Jewish circles, Roger Waters has become almost as well known for his antizionism as for his music. Viewed by many as the celebrity leader of the cultural boycott campaign against Israel, he seems to work feverishly to cajole, intimidate, and browbeat his fellow artists into following suit.

Waters's opening salvo to artists is typically a personal, sometimes private, communiqué dripping with what I find to be false humility. He expresses his admiration for their professional work and compliments them on their social justice causes before excoriating Israel and offering up what appears to be a thinly veiled threat to their reputation.[132] Waters's private pleas then degrade into personal attacks on public pages because, like Glenn Close in *Fatal Attraction*, Roger Waters will *not* be ignored.

In 2015, Roger Waters wrote to nine-time Grammy nominee Alan Parsons of the Alan Parsons Project hoping to persuade him to cancel an upcoming concert date in Israel. Alan had been an EMI Records engineer, and the two of them worked together on the album *Dark Side of the Moon*. The email began: "It's been 40 years since we worked on *Dark Side of the Moon* together. If you recall, I was the pimply bass player, you were the tall engineer. Congratulations on your many successes since then."[133] Kinda sweet, right? Not for long.

When Parsons declined to cancel his performance in Israel, Waters ignored his request to keep their exchange private and posted about it on Facebook. Parsons later described the exchange to the *Jerusalem Post* as "a little bit of conflict going on over the Internet."[134] The two have not spoken since.

Other times, when it appears his saccharine fawning will not warm hearts, Waters cuts straight to the chase. In 2015, Jon Bon Jovi announced his band's first concert date in Tel Aviv by saying, "Always heard what a wonderful place Israel is—the birthplace of all religions. I have been everywhere and Israel was a place that I've always wanted to visit, but it never worked out. This time I insisted that Israel must be on our list and it happened!"[135]

As reported on ISRAEL21c, when asked about Waters and his controversial boycott campaign to get other singers to nix concerts in Israel, Bon Jovi responded, "Yes, I heard about that but it doesn't interest me. I told my managers to give one simple answer: That I'm coming to Israel and I'm excited to come."[136]

In response, Waters published a scathing open letter in Salon. com demonizing both the Jewish homeland and the band that was subsequently picked up by *Rolling Stone* magazine. It is loaded with inflammatory innuendo and falsely depicts the Jews of Israel as pure evil, reading in part, "You stand shoulder to shoulder…With the bulldozer driver who crushed Rachel Corrie."[137]

Waters is referring to a young American anti-Israel activist who placed herself in harm's way by stepping in front of a moving bulldozer. Her tragic death was an accident, not an act of Israeli depravity, as Waters suggests.[138]

Israel protects the rights of its citizens and others to peacefully protest the government and actions of its military. Waters, and those who have lionized this young woman, fail to acknowledge that protest in Israel can be effective and safe. Corrie's death was tragic but entirely avoidable.

Waters's emotionally manipulative imagery seems intended to incite hate against these Jewish "monsters" and justify the destruction of the Jewish homeland. Why should the world tolerate such evil people in its midst? Disgracefully, he paints Bon Jovi with the same despicable brush.

WATERS'S CENTRAL TENETS

Based on his public statements and actions, it appears to me that Waters has convinced himself of a few central themes or beliefs to justify his crusade to condemn the Jewish people in Israel.

Israelis do not want peace. In Waters's syllogism, if Israelis do not want peace, then they deserve a collective punishment, are responsible for their government's policies, cannot be persuaded through dialogue, and are capable of monstrous and inhuman acts. Therefore, Waters must bolster his claim that Israelis do not want peace (despite their repeated offers—and Palestinian steadfast refusal—to trade land for peace) to justify what, in my opinion, is his hate mongering.

Walls are always bad, and there is something wrong with the people who build them. In 2002, Israel began building a security barrier to prevent Palestinian suicide bombers from murdering civilians during the Second Intifada, and Waters called for it to be taken down. Apparently, he does not recognize the difference between keeping citizens who want to emigrate locked in, as was the case of the Berlin Wall in Germany, and keeping terrorists out, as is the case in Israel.

In the opening sequence of the documentary *Walled Horizons*, which he narrates, he says, "The reason for walls is always fear, whether it's the personal walls we build around ourselves or walls like this,"[139] alluding to the fence.

Waters sees Israel's security barrier as the result of a psychological and irrational Israeli fear that they must themselves overcome. In an interview with Gideon Levy for *Haaretz*, he recalls a childhood memory about his mother's friend, a French-Jewish Holocaust survivor with a number tattooed on her forearm:[140]

I remember she was terrified for her children. Her kids were not allowed to come out in a canoe with us. You can imagine. Well, you can't, none of us can imagine. But I remember that, I remember thinking, *Why is this woman scared of the river?* You know, she was scared of everything; she was scared of her own shadow.

He discounts that before the security barrier existed, thousands of Israeli mothers, fathers, and children were killed in coffee shops, pizza parlors, and on buses during the two intifadas. If only they were just a little braver.

Waters is the victim here. Waters seems to believe he is the victim of the all-powerful Jews. He claims that the "Israeli lobby" not only stalks the halls of government but the recording studios of the music industry. In an interview for *CounterPunch*, Waters says it has been difficult to get other people, including artists, to care about people who are different from themselves. This, of course, he also blames on the Jews, saying it "has been a very hard sell particularly where I live in the United States of America. The Jewish lobby is extraordinarily powerful here and particularly in the industry that I work in, the music industry and in rock'n roll as they say." And, according to Waters, "I promise you, naming no names, I've spoken to people who are terrified that if they stand shoulder to shoulder with me they are going to get f**ked. They have said to me 'aren't you worried for your life?' and I go 'No, I'm not.'"[141]

To stand by these beliefs, Waters ignores Palestinian terrorism and Israeli suffering and absolves Palestinians of any responsibility for the hostilities. He stirs up animosity and fails to call for peace or reconciliation. Instead, he paints an unfounded black-and-white picture and declares that anyone who does not side with his version of good must be evil.

Radio host and personality Howard Stern has publicly called out Waters for his incessant attacks on the Jewish homeland. Stern asks:[142]

> Where's the one place they can stick Jews where no one will be offended? Because the Jews are getting killed all over the world. Give them a little homeland on a desert where there's no water, where essentially no one could live. And no one did live there despite the b******t. And the Palestinians are these Arabs that could live in Egypt, that could live in Saudi Arabia...Israel has a tiny little country and it bugs the s**t out of Roger Waters.

SO, HOW DID THIS ALL START?

Many people, including Waters himself, would point to a 2006 visit to Israel as a turning point in his journey, but his ruminations about isolation, walls, and the Middle East began before then.

Extreme politics is in his blood. Both his parents were Communists and supported far-left causes. His father, who died when Waters was a baby (fighting Nazis, as he likes to say), sympathized with the Arabs during skirmishes with the Jews when he taught in Jerusalem between 1936 and 1938. According to what he said in an interview in *Haaretz*, Waters was taken in by a Lebanese family as a young man and touched by their graciousness.[143]

From 1977 to 1979, Waters wrote Pink Floyd's concept album *The*

Wall. The song "Another Brick in the Wall" was a metaphor for the alienation he felt from his audience. In the late '80s, Waters campaigned to take down the Berlin Wall in East Germany.

In 2002, he objected to Israel's security barrier, but his objection to walls is not universal. He does not seem concerned with the dozens of other walls that are built between people, including those between India and Pakistan, Iran and Afghanistan, and Iran and other countries, like Saudi Arabia. Nor is he interested in bringing down the so-called "Peace Walls" that continue to separate Catholics and Protestants in Northern Ireland.

In 2006, Waters booked an Israel concert with promoter Shuki Weiss at Tel Aviv's HaYarkon Park. Despite his objection to the barrier, he had not yet endorsed the boycott that had begun two years earlier, and the BDS campaign criticized him harshly.

Initially, he refused to back down. "I have a lot of fans in Israel, many of whom are refuseniks. I would not rule out going to Israel because I disapprove of the foreign policy any more than I would refuse to play in the UK because I disapprove of Tony Blair's foreign policy...I am happy to play to anybody who believes in peace. I don't discriminate between any of my fans, wherever they live. Being an Israeli does not disbar from being a human being."[144]

However, just before the concert, he met with BDS co-founder Omar Barghouti, who persuaded him to question his thinking. The relationship, which continues to this day, has been a key to Waters's journey down the rabbit hole.

Waters was escorted on a tour of Bethlehem with a stop at a

segment of the barrier that is a cement wall. Contrary to anti-Israel propaganda, only a very small section of the barrier is concrete; 90–95 percent is chain-link fence. Concrete structures are built in locations "where there is a history of snipers shooting at Israeli civilians, and along the outskirts of municipal Jerusalem."[145] Moved by the experience, Waters doubled down on his anti-wall sentiment and spray-painted the lyric "We don't need no thought control" on the wall. Exactly what that means in this context is unclear. In Israel, as opposed to in Hamas-controlled Gaza and in the West Bank, there is no "thought control" going on. Nonetheless, the image has become emblematic for BDS proponents.

Still uncertain about the boycott, Waters decided to move the concert rather than cancel it. The new site was a chickpea farm halfway between Tel Aviv and Jerusalem, outside a village called Neve Shalom, which means "Oasis of Peace." In Neve Shalom, Jewish, Christian, and Palestinian Israelis farm the land together in cooperation and harmony.

Approximately fifty thousand people attended what many have described as Israel's Woodstock. The last-minute change in location created logistical chaos and three-hour traffic jams, but the band and the enthusiastic crowd had a great time. A few years later, however, Waters recast the experience as a disturbing glimpse into the Israeli heart.

By 2009, he still had not officially endorsed the boycott but was forming increasingly closer ties with Israel's detractors, including Barghouti and UNRWA, which arranged a visit for him to Jenin in the West Bank. Later, he admitted the town was "much livelier and modern" than he had imagined,[146] a fact he does not like to repeat. Immediately following the Jenin visit, Waters spoke at the Sam Spiegel Film and Television School in Jerusalem and warned the students there that many no longer believe the Jewish people deserve a state of their own.

In 2010, Waters began the *Wall Live* tour, using the antisemitic symbols noted earlier as part of his stage show.

By 2011, Waters saw the message of "Another Brick in the Wall" as an analogy to the way ideologists, governments, and religions react to one another.[147] He announced his official membership in the BDS campaign and called for his brothers and sisters in the arts to join him.[148] In 2012, he became a member of the Russell Tribunal on Palestine, which has no legal status but acts—according to its website—as a court of the people. Unsurprisingly, the Russell Tribunal has declared Israel an apartheid state.

By 2013, Waters's conversion to BDS apostle was complete. He reissued the call to boycott in a *Rolling Stone* piece by Jon Blistein, launching his new career as the "poster boy" for the campaign and saying a boycott similar to the one implemented against South Africa during apartheid was the "way to go."[149]

Waters portrays himself as a champion of justice, but many artists, including Israeli Guy Erez, bass player for the Alan Parsons Live Project, question his intent:[150]

> If Roger Waters really wanted to be a peaceful person, why won't he take a group of Israeli kids and Palestinian kids and make a camp of making music together. Use the power of music to put people together. But don't just say, "I'm taking a side. Don't

share music with the Israeli people." Why do the Israeli people or any other people have to get punished even though let's say you disagree with their government? It's just something I don't understand how he even puts it together.

David Draiman, lead singer of heavy metal band Disturbed, has also weighed in with his opinion:[151]

> The very notion that Waters and the rest of his Nazi comrades decide that this is the way to go ahead and foster change is absolute lunacy and idiocy. It makes no sense whatsoever. It's only based on hatred of a culture and of a people in a society that has been demonized unjustifiably since the beginning of time.

To cling to his beliefs yet rationalize his behavior, Waters must reassign truths. In 2006, he had nothing negative to say about the concert at Neve Shalom, but now, Waters points to a moment during the concert as evidence of Israel's bellicose character.

According to Waters, toward the end of the show, he asked the audience to be the generation that leads the way to peace and "suddenly the crowd went silent." Waters tells this story in interview after interview and speech after speech to support his claim that Israelis do not want peace, and therefore, there is no point in international artists going to Israel to try to stimulate dialogue. The point was not missed by journalist Larry Derfner, who wrote in *+972 Magazine*:[152]

> This is a very popular idea—that foreign artists, scientists and others who oppose the occupation shouldn't stay away, but rather come to Israel and "engage," try to change people's minds. Waters' recollection of his 2006 concert in front of 45,000 Israelis

addresses that point—and also says something about the young generation here, and about how rock music doesn't set everyone free.

Of all the tall tales that Waters has told, that must be the tallest. It is clear from a video recording of the concert posted by *The Times of Israel* blogger David Seidenberg that he did not simply urge the audience to make peace with their neighbors but to also "tear down the walls."* He not only misstates the quote but seems to lie about the reaction. As can be clearly seen and heard on video, the crowd broke into loud cheers and applause.[153] In interviews after the concert, members of the young audience were happy to discuss Waters's remarks.[154] Some said they wanted peace but were concerned that if the barrier came down, many more Israelis would die. The audience did not fall silent, as Waters has claimed. It was supportive of peace and open to dialogue, but some were rationally concerned about attacks if the security barrier was removed.

Waters also uses that concert experience as validation for his unfounded claim that Israeli cultural events are segregated. "Afterward, I thought about the implications of travel restrictions and realized it was pretty unlikely that there were any Palestinians or Arabs in the audience, and I felt really bad about that."[155] And "it was very strange performing to a completely segregated audience because there were no Palestinians there. There were just 60,000 Jewish Israelis, who could not have been more welcoming, nice and loyal to Pink Floyd. Nevertheless, it left an uncomfortable feeling."[156]

---

* He said, "And, I may be speaking out of turn, but I believe that we, the rest of the world, need this generation of Israelis to tear down the walls and to make peace with their neighbors."

Israel has restrictions on Palestinians entering Israel from the West Bank for security reasons, but that certainly does not mean there were no Arab Israelis in the audience. If Waters is suggesting Arab Israelis are turned away at the gate because of ethnic discrimination, that is untrue. The fact is anybody in Israel is free to purchase a ticket to a concert. If he is suggesting they cannot, as a group,* afford tickets to his concert, perhaps he should lower his prices.

PUSH BACK

Just as Waters is free to express his political opinions, so is everyone else. However, unlike Waters, who creates de facto blacklists galore to advance his agenda, and contrary to his insinuations, there has been no effort within the industry to blacklist or oust him. Waters continues to tour and perform.

Outside the entertainment industry, yes, there have been boycott campaigns, although surprisingly few given the damage he seemingly seeks to sow.

In November 2017, five German state television and radio affiliates of the national ARD network announced the cancellation of scheduled public broadcastings of Waters's performances following accusations of antisemitism and his campaigning on behalf of BDS.[157]

Also in 2017, a Miami Beach teen club rejected an invitation to participate in Waters's *Us + Them* tour. A spokesperson for

---

* Both the Arab Muslim and Orthodox Jewish populations are among the poorest groups in the nation.

Miami Beach said, "Miami Beach is a culturally diverse community and does not tolerate any form of hate."[158]

In February 2020, Major League Baseball (MLB) ran promotions for Waters's upcoming North American tour *This Is Not a Drill*. Following criticism from Jewish advocacy groups, including B'nai B'rith, which wrote a letter to MLB's commissioner, Rob Manfred, saying Waters's views on Israel "far exceed the boundaries of civil discourse,"[159] MLB stopped running the promotions.

Other anti–Roger Waters protests did not bring about a cancellation but successfully brought attention to his blatant antisemitism. In 2017, the Jewish Community Relations Council of Greater Washington circulated a video criticizing Waters ahead of his scheduled concerts in Washington, DC. Activists in other cities, such as Nashville and Philadelphia, also targeted his upcoming shows with protests.

When asked in a 2020 interview about his response to those who ask him to, in his words, "Shut the f*** up and stick to music," he said both ironically and arrogantly, "No! You're not an artist, you shut the f*** up...How dare you think you have an influence on my life...You're a nobody."[160]

Few artists cave under Waters's bullying and pressure to cancel. Some fight back, while most thankfully ignore his noise. Unfortunately, that does not mean Waters has completely failed. American journalist Alan Light, who has been a rock critic for *Rolling Stone* and the editor in chief for both *Vibe* and *Spin*, summed up Waters's efforts this way:[161]

You're trying to largely use this as a way to draw attention to the cause. And we're here and we're talking about it, so to that extent, what Pink Floyd has done still counts as a success.

NEXT STEP: MOCK ROGER WATERS.

Why? Because it will bug him. Call him an antisemite if you believe he is one.

CHAPTER TEN

BDS ZEALOTS

"Israel must become a pariah state."

—KEN LOACH, BRITISH DIRECTOR

The cultural boycott campaign against Israel is a censorship campaign. The fact that it is happening is alarming. That it is supported by artists is unimaginable.

As previously noted, very few artists support the cultural boycott of Israel. Fewer still have made it a personal crusade. I refer to those who have as "BDS Zealots."

In free, open societies like the US and Israel, each of us has the right to choose for ourselves what we want to see and hear based on our politics and taste. However, in the case of BDS Zealots, we are not dealing with individuals who are merely making personal choices. Instead, we are dealing with artists who are seeking to bend the entire creative community to their will and intimidate everyone who disagrees with their political agenda.

Much of the "zeal" of these artists appears to be tied to their progressive politics and, in the case of the UK, their attachment to far-left voices inside the Labour Party, particularly former leader Jeremy Corbyn. In recent years, Labour, which has been the political home to Jews in the UK for generations, has found itself embroiled in charges of antisemitism.

In October 2020, the human rights watchdog the Equality and Human Rights Commission found Labour responsible for "unlawful" harassment and discrimination against its Jewish members during Mr. Corbyn's four and a half years as leader. Responding to the report, party member Sir Keir Starmer said it was "a day of shame for the Labour Party" and apologized to the Jewish community. On the other hand, the response on the part of some of these Zealots, as you will see, was indignation.

BDS Zealots work primarily in the public square and use their celebrity as a bully pulpit. They claim to be human rights advocates and protectors of children. In addition to signing group statements, they write personal letters that are picked up by mainstream media. They participate in BDS videos and seize opportunities in interviews and speaking engagements to expound on the subject. They are quick to engage on social media. They pressure friends and associates to boycott. They endorse anti-Israel grassroots organizations. They propagate BDS messaging in their art.

The intensity of the emotion aimed at the Jewish state for its perceived wrongdoings far exceeds the condemnation by these Zealots of the horrors and tragedies taking place against the Uighurs in China, the Rohingya in Myanmar, or the Darfur genocide in Sudan, among many others.

Many BDS Zealots are Arab artists who support the cultural boycott campaign for personal reasons fueled by the intergenerational conflict between Arabs and Jews. They are unlikely to be swayed by any social media campaign that we can devise. We need to focus our attention elsewhere—on BDS Zealots from the West.

In my view, some of the most active Zealots include Roger Waters (whom we have already discussed) as well as such artists as Brian Eno, Thurston Moore, Caryl Churchill, the late Alan Rickman, Ken Loach, Alice Walker, Lauryn Hill, Danny Glover, Banksy, and Remy.

BRIAN ENO

Englishman Brian Eno is a widely respected music composer, artist, and producer best known for his ambient sounds and for working with bands such as Talking Heads, U2, and Coldplay.

Eno shares Waters's rabid antizionist politics and is one of the most outspoken artists championing the BDS campaign against Israel. He is a signatory to the APUK pledge to boycott the Jewish homeland and has publicly attacked other artists who have performed in Israel, such as Nick Cave and Thom Yorke.

As early as 2009, Eno gave an anti-Israel speech at a London rally dubbed "Stop Gaza Massacre." In that speech, Eno compared the Israelis to Nazis, saying, "By creating a Middle Eastern version of the Warsaw ghetto they [the Jews] are recapitulating their own history as though they've forgotten it." He called the Israelis "a gifted and resourceful people" ("resourceful" often being a code word for the antisemitic aspersion of "cunning" or "crafty" Jews) and said, "It's difficult to avoid the conclusion that this conflict serves the political and economic purposes of Israel" (economic purposes being a way to say that money is what drives Israelis). Eno concluded with a "thieving" Jew inference, "And then you [Israelis] can carry on with business as usual, quietly stealing their [the Palestinian] homeland."[162]

He wrote a letter to Talking Heads' David Byrne, which Byrne posted on his website and *Billboard* magazine republished. The letter compares Israelis to the Ku Klux Klan and labels Israel "a ragingly racist theocracy." Eno describes Jews from certain parts of the world as interlopers: "Most of them are not ethnic Israelis—they're 'right of return' Jews from Russia and Ukraine."[163]

Byrne, to his credit, published a response to the letter from his friend Peter Schwartz, who pointed out:[164]

> I find the opposition to Israel questionable in its failure to be similarly outraged by a vast number of other moral horrors in the recent past and currently active. Just to name a few[;] Cambodia, Tibet, Sudan, Somalia, Nicaragua, Mexico, Argentina, Liberia, Central African Republic, Uganda, North Korea, Bosnia, Kosovo, Venezuela, Syria, Egypt, Libya, Zimbabwe[,] and especially right now Nigeria.

In 2020, Eno was interviewed with Roger Waters on Frank Barat's podcast.[165] Barat is a French BDS activist, author, and film producer. From 2008 to 2014, he was the coordinator of the Russell Tribunal on Palestine. He has edited books with prominent figures who similarly castigate Israel, including Noam Chomsky, Ilan Pappé, Ken Loach, and Angela Davis. He was part of the founding team of the Festival Ciné-Palestine in Paris and the Palestine with Love Festival in Brussels, the latter of which celebrates the "cinema of resistance."

Although Barat's interview with Waters and Eno was supposedly about music and politics in the COVID-19 world, it did not take long for it to stray to the three participants' love-to-hate topic: Israel. When Barat asked why there are so few musicians and other artists supporting BDS, Eno offered three potential explanations, which I summarize as follows:

Artists who perform in Israel are in it for the money. Artists perform in Israel for the same reason they do everywhere else— because they love what they do, and yes, they get paid, some better than others. Why does Eno single out performances in the Jewish homeland and connect them to greed, a classic antisemitic trope?

These artists are cowards; they are afraid of being called antisemitic. So, artists are afraid of being called antisemitic but not afraid of being called racist or war criminals, the labels he and his ilk dish out? Absurd.

And lastly, *They are naïve. They honestly believe that art is always good, and therefore, the best thing they can do is carry on making it.* Unlike the first two explanations, this one is true.

Cultural exchange builds bridges between people. The artists who reject the cultural boycott recognize that people are much more likely to like one another when they feel they have something in common, and art and music can provide that commonality. The Iranian picture that won the Oscar for Best Foreign Language Film in 2012, *A Separation,* was about a divorcing couple dealing with an aging father suffering from Alzheimer's disease. This universal predicament played out within a distinct culture allowed the audience to connect with the characters on an emotional level and humanized the citizenry of a country many nations and individuals view as an enemy.

The United States and many European countries impose economic sanctions on Iran, which exports international terror and regularly calls for the destruction of the United States and Israel. However, no one suggested (or should suggest) that the world boycott this film because it was made by an Iranian filmmaker. Yet, if the filmmaker were Israeli, there would certainly have been a call for a boycott by BDS Zealots.

THURSTON MOORE

Thurston Moore is an American guitarist who founded the '80s noise rock band Sonic Youth. Moore's progressive political activism has included opposing US incursions into the Middle East and signing a letter in support of Jeremy Corbyn's English Labour Party when it was accused of mistreating its Jewish members.

Sonic Youth played Tel Aviv in 1996. At the time, Moore said, "It was an amazing, wonderful experience and education."[166] However, in April 2015, Moore canceled a scheduled performance in Tel Aviv without explanation. Two months later, he published a statement in a British online music and pop culture magazine that said in part, "It was with serious deliberation that I eventually arrived at the personal conclusion that to perform with my band in Israel was in direct conflict to my values."[167]

Ever since, Moore has been a BDS Zealot who can be counted on to sign the campaign's open letters and petitions. In 2020, he publicly called on American rock band Dinosaur Jr. to cancel its Israeli show in an open letter:[168]

> The power is in your heart, mind and soul to stand up against the Israel state-sanctioned violence of extremist, racist, sexist nationalism. We, who support this movement, are not interested in "bullying" anyone to not accept opportunities of work, or is it a suggestion towards the beauty that is the citizenry of Israel, it is just asking, by any PEACE-ful means necessary, to aid the oppressed from the oppressor.

Israel is sexist? When millions of the world's women live in oppressive conditions, unable to walk outside without a man accompanying them or forced to cover themselves head to toe to hide from the gaze of men, with little legal, marital, or property rights, Moore singles out Israel? Israel, which was the third country in the world to have a democratically elected female leader (something the US has yet to have) and has women serving in every branch of the military and the political system as well as serving in the judiciary—including on the Supreme Court—is sexist?

This unfounded demonizing makes sense when you see Israel through the antisemitic association of Jews and evil. Moore makes this ridiculous charge because—like extremism, racism, and nationalism—he considers sexism bad, and therefore, it must exist in Israel.

Not only does BDS constantly invent new accusations against the Jewish state, but its favorite tactic is to find Israel guilty of those wrongs that are practiced without restraint in other nations as well as by the PA and in Gaza under the Hamas-led government.

Suffice it to say, Moore's comments seem to be symptomatic of the self-delusion that afflicts BDS supporters. If he believes that BDS does not "bully others" or that it recognizes the "beauty" of Israeli citizens, he is likely living in an alternate universe. "Extremist, racist, sexist nationalism" does not describe Israeli society—but it certainly does describe Hamas's rule in Gaza.

CARYL CHURCHILL

Caryl Churchill is a popular British playwright whose work, most notably *Cloud Nine* and *Top Girls*, has had long runs in off-Broadway theaters in New York. Her works often deal with political issues such as gender and power.

Churchill is a longtime patron of the Palestine Solidarity Campaign (PSC),[169] a group that supports the boycott of Israel and organizes many of the anti-Israel protests at the Festival Fringe in Edinburgh. Churchill wrote a ten-minute play called *Seven Jewish Children,* which purports to tell the history of Israel from its founding to the 2018 Gaza War in a series of vignettes in which Israeli parents are deciding whether or not to tell their children "the truth" of what Israel has done.

Seven Jewish Children was widely denounced as antisemitic. The *Sunday Times* condemned its "ludicrous and utterly predictable lack of even-handedness."[170] Churchill is among those who have not acknowledged antisemitism in the Labour Party and has signed a petition in support of party leader Jeremy Corbyn.

ALAN RICKMAN

Classically trained member of the Royal Shakespeare Company and Golden Globe-, Emmy-, and BAFTA-winning British actor, the late Alan Rickman came to fame as the villain in the first *Die Hard* movie. He gained even more recognition by playing Severus Snape in the *Harry Potter* films and Emma Thompson's straying husband in *Love Actually*.

Although some assumed Rickman was Jewish, he was of Catholic and Methodist background. In 2005, along with journalist Katharine Viner (who would go on to become editor in chief of *The Guardian,* a left-leaning publication), Rickman compiled and directed a play called *My Name Is Rachel Corrie*. The play is based on the diaries and emails of Rachel Corrie, the American college student who traveled to the Gaza Strip as an anti-Israel activist during the Second Intifada. As previously discussed, Corrie died in Gaza when she stepped in front of an IDF bulldozer that was demolishing a building containing tunnels terrorists used to move illegal weapons and explosives and carry out attacks on Israel.

Although the bulldozer operator could not see Corrie, Palestinian activists claimed that she was run over intentionally. Corrie has since been portrayed as a martyr for the Palestinian cause and an example of Israel's willingness to murder innocent people.

Viner and Rickman's play was first staged in April 2005 at London's Royal Court Theatre. Despite criticism in the press over its one-sided viewpoint that ignored Palestinian terrorism, the play won several British theater awards.

Although Rickman passed away in 2016, his play continues to

be performed and, in my estimation, perpetuates a grisly and unfounded blood libel against the Israeli people.

KEN LOACH

Another Brit who has found his way to antizionism is Palme d'Or–winning director Ken Loach, whose films showcase the political and social experiences of the working class. His film *I Daniel Blake* won the Palme d'Or at Cannes in 2016 and the BAFTA Award for Best British Film in 2017. In an impassioned speech at the Sarajevo Film Festival in 2014, he called for an "absolute boycott of all the cultural happenings supported by the Israeli state" and declared that "Israel must become a pariah state."[171]

Loach is an active member of APUK and has picked public fights with artists such as Thom Yorke for playing in Israel. In 2017, Yorke fired back, saying:[172]

> Playing in a country isn't the same as endorsing its government. We've played in Israel for over 20 years through a succession of governments, some more liberal than others. We do not endorse Netanyahu any more than Trump, but we still play in America. Music, art, and academia is about crossing borders not building them, about open minds not closed ones, about shared humanity, dialogue[,] and freedom of expression. I hope that makes it clear[,] Ken.

Ironically, a 2018 article in *The Guardian* revealed that Loach did not seem to feel the boycott applied to his own films, which have successfully been released in Israel since 1995. When confronted with this likely hypocrisy, Loach's producer, Rebecca O'Brien, claimed his film was accidentally sold to Israel and that Loach did not know.[173]

Loach's Israeli distributor, Guy Shani, replied:[174]

> I can't tell you how absurd this is. We've been showing his movies for years. I have been paying him money every year…You don't sell a film to someone a director doesn't want a film sold to. It is a serious business. You have a list of regions and they approve country by country and then you need to get approval by producer and director. And if you have a relationship, a sales agent with a director who is really important to you, of course you don't sell against their wishes.

Loach is also an apologist for antisemitism within the British Labour Party. In 2018, he urged the party to suspend thirty MPs who appeared at a rally to end antisemitism, while he opposed the removal of other party members who espoused antisemitic views, saying, "We've never had a leader like Corbyn before in the whole history of the Labour Party…and that's why the dirty tricks [a seeming code for devious Jews] are going to come out."[175]

In 2019, Loach objected to the airing of a BBC current-affairs documentary titled *Is Labour Anti-Semitic?*[176] and wrote to BAFTA urging it to reconsider the decision to nominate it for an award.

In August 2021, the Labour Party finally addressed the situation, and Loach was given the option of either denouncing those already expelled or to be expelled himself. He chose the latter.[177]

ALICE WALKER

Among the most entrenched BDS Zealots is American novelist Alice Walker. In 1983, Walker made history as the first female African American to win the Pulitzer Prize for literature as well as the National Book Award for fiction for her novel *The Color Purple*. Set in the American South in the early twentieth century, this much-beloved book details the cultural and social oppression of Black Americans through the lives of Black women.

Walker banned the translation of the novel into Hebrew and wrote an open letter to Alicia Keys pleading with her to cancel her upcoming concert in Israel. (More on this letter later.)

Walker also praised in the *New York Times* the book *And the Truth Shall Set You Free* by the British conspiracist David Icke.[178] The book theorizes about Jewish extraterrestrial forces that control the world, an apparent antisemitic trope of Jewish omnipotence. Walker called it a "curious person's dream come true."[179]

LAURYN HILL

Ms. Lauryn Hill, an American singer, songwriter, and rapper, abruptly canceled her scheduled performance in Israel following intense pressure by the BDS campaign. At the time, Hill explained the cancellation on Facebook by saying she intended to perform in both Israel and the West Bank, but since that was not possible, "It is very important to me that my presence or message not be misconstrued, or a source of alienation to either my Israeli or my Palestinian fans."[180] Her Facebook post ended with the following wish: "May healing, equanimity, and the openness necessary for lasting resolution and reconciliation come to this region and its people."[181]

Just months later, however, when Israelis were suffering under bloody attacks from a slew of knife-wielding terrorists, she did an about-face and participated in an incendiary video, "When I See Them, I See Us,"[182] that, in my opinion, falsely equated the Israeli–Palestinian conflict with simmering tensions between Black Americans and police forces in the United States.[183] Known Israel detractors Angela Davis, Dr. Cornel West, Alice Walker, Danny Glover, and Omar Barghouti also participated in the video, awash with inflammatory rhetoric such as, "They burned me alive in Jerusalem."

DANNY GLOVER

Danny Glover is a Black American actor best known for his work as Mel Gibson's down-to-earth police partner in the *Lethal Weapon* film series.

Glover participated in a documentary about Grace Lee Boggs, a Chinese American philosopher and Marxist ideologist who was a force in the Civil Rights and Black Power movements in America. Despite Boggs's anti-Israel politics, the film was accepted into the Docaviv International Documentary Film Festival in Tel Aviv. Just days before the film was scheduled to screen, Glover joined William Ayers, a leader of the 1960s radical group Weather Underground, and rapper Invincible to issue a statement that called for the film to be withdrawn. Unfortunately for these advocates, it was too late for it to be removed from the schedule.

The fact that the Docaviv International Documentary Film Festival chose to screen a film that champions the life and work of a feminist Israel-detractor is itself a sign of Israel's open and pluralistic society and undermines many of BDS's accusations. As a self-described feminist, one would think that Boggs, and her admirers, would take note that Golda Meir, Israel's fourth prime minister, was one of the world's most respected democratically elected female leaders and that in the ethnically and racially diverse Israel, beauty comes in many colors. Yityish Titi Aynaw, Miss Israel 2013, was born in Ethiopia and, in response to a judge's question, had this to say: "There are many different communities of many different colors in Israel, and it's important to show that to the world."[184]

BANKSY

Banksy is a much-revered England-based political street artist and documentary filmmaker who has sold his work for millions. Banksy's shtick is to keep his identity anonymous by pixilating his face in photographs or turning his back to the camera. A hoodie-wearing, middle-aged multimillionaire known for subversive epigrams and theatrical pranks—he once programmed a piece of his artwork to self-shred just as it was being auctioned off—Banksy has aimed his poison brush at Israel.

The security barrier that runs through Bethlehem is awash in his murals romanticizing Palestinian terrorism and portraying Palestinian residents in the area as peaceful freedom fighters and innocent victims. One mural, for example, depicts a militant throwing a bouquet of flowers instead of a rock, and another shows a young girl being pulled upward by balloons to transcend the barrier.[185]

In 2014, Banksy released a two-minute mockumentary in the style of a tourism video facetiously urging the viewer to consider vacation plans in Gaza.[186] Emotionally manipulative and devoid of context, the camera documents the region's war-torn buildings but ignores the rockets fired at Israeli cities. It showcases the illegal Hamas tunnels into Israel as if they function to keep people out of Gaza rather than being used by Palestinian terrorists as roadways to murder innocent Israeli civilians. There are shots of children playing in rubble but no footage of the thousands of greenhouses that were left behind by the Israelis, which Hamas chose to destroy rather than use to feed the Palestinian people.

In 2017, Banksy was a driving force behind the construction of a Bethlehem tourist destination and fully functioning colonial-themed lodge called the Walled Off Hotel. Each of the rooms contains his artwork, and the hotel boasts a small museum and serves an English high tea in the afternoon.

Most reviewers on Tripadvisor rave about the excellent food and local beauty, with one traveler describing the visit as "a dream come true." The graffiti-covered security wall also gets praise as one reviewer writes, "Words fail…has to be seen to be believed. Just do it!!! Nothing can compare to enjoying a pot of Earl Grey tea while enjoying the worst view in the world"[187] Perhaps in hopes of indoctrinating guests to the cause, the hotel invites them to add their own artwork to the wall during their stay.

Although Jewish Israelis do not have safe passage in and out of Bethlehem, many of the hotel visitors describe how easy it is for non-Israelis to go back and forth between the locations.

REMY

In 2020, Navajo artist, Remy, put up several murals based on images found in the news media on an adobe wall in Santa Fe's Historic Eastside district, which cast Israelis as oppressors. The emotionally laden papier-mâché installations included one of twelve-year-old Mohammad al-Dura, who was allegedly shot in a Palestinian–Israeli crossfire at the beginning of the Second Intifada in 2000. Although the young boy has become a martyr for the Palestinian cause, the incident has been hotly contested with some questioning not only who may have shot him, but whether he was shot at all.[188]

The artist says he lived with a Palestinian family in 2011 who made comparisons between themselves and the indigenous people of America, no doubt failing to mention that Jews too are indigenous people whose roots in the region are more than three thousand years old.

A local Jewish leader, Rabbi Levertov, said the intention of the murals was "not to promote peace, but to instigate and inspire hate. And in today's environment with the rise in antisemitism, this is not serving any goodness in the world."[189]

Reflecting the fears of many in the Jewish community, local resident Richard Lieberman asked:[190]

> I have to drive by this wall every day? It's antisemitic. It plays into age-old dangerous and false anti-Jewish tropes. Here we are, 75 years after the liberation of Auschwitz, and we are facing an uptick in dangerous rhetoric that reminds us of those dark times. What we fear is that after the murals come the swastikas.

* * *

When it comes to the Jews, BDS Zealots transform a complex reality into an archetypical battle between good and evil. To them, this is a holy war, and they are the righteous. As a consequence, many fail to recognize the ethical (and potentially legal) difference between expressing an opinion and harassing and intimidating those who disagree.

While we may not be able to change the hearts of the most devoted Zealots, we can put them on the defense by exposing the antisemitic tropes beneath their rhetoric. We do not have to organize boycott campaigns against them. Once the veil is lifted, event organizers and audiences may do that on their own.

More important than any cancellation or counter boycott, however, is to invite scrutiny of the underlying message of their words and actions. If they traffic in antisemtic tropes and foment Jew-hatred, there must be consequences for them in the court of public opinion.

NEXT STEP: CHALLENGE ZEALOTS.

Go on the offensive. Do not worry about people accusing you of playing "the antisemitism card."

Remember when the charge that someone was playing the "race card" silenced them? When was the last time that happened?

CHAPTER ELEVEN

THE CONTINUUM

*"There's an awful lot of people who don't agree
with the BDS movement, including us."*

—THOM YORKE, RADIOHEAD SINGER AND SONGWRITER

Although BDS makes much hay about every concert cancellation, and groups on both sides often see the issue in terms of black and white, artist support for the cultural boycott of Israel is really a continuum. On one end are BDS Zealots, followed by Israel Bashers, leading eventually on the other end to Unwitting Accomplices (i.e., those artists who have been completely misrepresented as BDS supporters but fail to correct the record).

ISRAEL BASHERS

As previously discussed, Israel Bashers, while falling short of a call to boycott, unfairly demonize the Jewish homeland and set the stage for the cultural boycott and worldwide Jew-hatred. While there appears to be some differences in motive (I do not think Jon Stewart would like to see the demise of Israel as a Jewish homeland, while Bella Hadid likely would), their antizionist hyperbole is the same.

Israel Bashers can be, and have been, persuaded to walk back their statements when they are exposed as thinly veiled Jew-hatred. Dozens of others have deleted their posts in the face of backlash or been forced to apologize or explain them. In 2021, Mark Ruffalo walked back an inference he made regarding Israeli genocide of the Palestinian people: "I have reflected & wanted to apologize for posts during the recent Israel/Hamas fighting that suggested Israel is committing 'genocide.' It's not accurate, it's inflammatory, disrespectful & is being used to justify antisemitism here & abroad. Now is the time to avoid hyperbole."[191] In the same year, Paris Hilton deleted a tweet in which she condemned the bombing of Gaza. Good. They need to know that there will be consequences for their disgraceful comments.

FELLOW TRAVELERS

What distinguishes a "Fellow Traveler" from a Zealot or Basher? Ferocity and frequency.

Fellow Travelers, like actors Julie Christie and Mark Rylance, will join BDS organizations, sign group statements, and make the occasional personal comment, but they are not preoccupied by the singling out of Israel. They make their impact by fostering the illusion that support for BDS in the artist community is widespread.

Most artists in this group, including APUK's 1,350 members, join the cause because of their progressive politics. My guess is that the majority have not read the BDS charter, nor do they care what is in it. Although the site is very active, most of its membership is not. Their contribution to the effort is signing the pledge. Many have never had, nor will they ever have, the opportunity to work in Israel, so a pledge to boycott it is mostly a symbolic gesture.

They believe they are on the "right side of history," but they are being misled by BDS lies.

Once we convince them they are associating with antisemites and backing anti-Jewish racism, their resolve will wane.

RELUCTANT SUPPORTERS

Reluctant Supporters are artists, like Lorde and Demi Lovato, who have bowed to BDS pressure and canceled scheduled trips or events with some sort of "apology" but do not champion the cause. These artists have been "converted by the sword" and feel they need to give a nod to the gods of cancel culture to save their reputations and careers. Although a few, like Lauryn Hill and Thurston Moore, become BDS Zealots, most are rarely heard from again.

I have great compassion for artists under fire and understand that some simply cannot stand the heat. We need to support them before they fold.

UNWITTING ACCOMPLICES

The far side of this continuum are artists like the Beach Boys who cancel for reasons unrelated to BDS but say nothing publicly when BDS claims that for a victory. Some of these artists, like Taylor Swift, never even booked a concert in Israel to begin with. Dismayed at the negative attention, it is understandable that they would want to drop the subject, but it is still wrong. Unless they publicly disavow the movement, their silence can be seen as complicity.

They need to follow the lead of many others, such as Lenny Kravitz, who had to cancel his concert because of a scheduling conflict and specifically denied the BDS false claim of victory that was reported in several publications, including *Agence France-Presse*. Kravitz wrote on Facebook:[192]

> I have been looking forward to performing in Israel for some time. The idea of ending my world tour there was also extremely meaningful to me. As a result I am personally disappointed and very sorry that my concert in Tel Aviv had to be postponed. I promise that I will be in Israel next year.

We must urge the Unwilling Accomplices to set the record straight.

NEXT STEP: FOCUS YOUR ENERGIES ON ARTISTS AND CELEBRITIES.

It is tempting to engage with every Tom, Dick, and Harry who is spreading lies about Israel (go ahead if you have the energy), but you will get the best bang for your buck when you engage with or talk about artists. See the upcoming chapter "Celebrities Make News."

On social media, other people will try to draw you in. If you feel compelled to respond, make sure you tag the celebrity, so they stay in the thread and remark to them how the conversation they started has devolved.

CHAPTER TWELVE

ANSWERING BDS

"Israel is a place that's managed to embrace its neighbors and create peace within an environment that can be very hostile."

—ASHTON KUTCHER, AMERICAN ACTOR

BDS campaigns are filled with damaging lies, half-truths, and cherry-picked facts without context, and attempting to discredit each one is a bit like a whack-a-mole arcade game; when you knock one down, another pops up. What lies at the foundation of BDS's most widespread and damaging charges? The classic antisemitic tropes discussed in Chapter Four.

GREEDY, THIEVING ISRAELIS: COLONIALISM AND STOLEN LANDS

BDS falsely characterizes Israelis as colonizers who have stolen Palestinian land. This canard plays on the antisemitic trope of greedy, thieving Jews gobbling up other people's wealth.

Colonialism refers to one nation dominating and subjugating another to reap the benefits of that country's land, resources, wealth, and workforce. BDS proponents are relying on the emotional resonance of the charge to get people feeling instead of asking questions. Members of the public often think that BDS is referring to the land now under dispute, including the West Bank settlements and East Jerusalem housing, but in fact, the BDS leadership is challenging the right of Israel to exist as a Jewish nation anywhere in the region.

As previously discussed, the Jews have a connection to the land going back thousands of years. The early Jewish pioneers of the late eighteenth and early nineteenth centuries purchased the land legally from its owners. They did not come on behalf of a foreign nation but to escape one. The Jews returned to this region, their ancestral homeland, because of their spiritual connection to the land; there was no wealth or resources to pillage.

Israel was recognized as an independent nation in 1948 by the UN just as numerous Arab nations had been a few years before.

The territory captured by Israel in 1967 is, at worst, disputed territory, not stolen territory. Israel gained that land in a defensive war and has a legitimate claim to it.

Professor Eugene Kontorovich of Northwestern's Pritzker School of Law testified before the US House of Representatives Subcommittee on National Security in 2018. In that testimony, he said the UN Charter distinguishes between aggressive wars, which are illegal, and defensive wars, which are not. The UN has repeatedly recognized territorial acquisition, and even annexation, as a result of a legal defensive war.

Today, the UN position on territorial acquisition resulting from *any* war might be changing, but in 1967, the rules were clear:[193]

Whatever the current status of an absolute prohibition on territorial change resulting from war, there was certainly no such blanket prohibition in 1967, when the territory came under Israeli control. At the time, international law only prohibited acquisition of force in illegal or aggressive wars.

There is much criticism today of the last several hundred years of colonialism by the West, and rightfully so. In the BDS analogy, however, Israelis are inaccurately pigeonholed as the "white occupiers" and Palestinians the ethnic victims.

Nothing could be further from the truth; Israel is a multi-ethnic democracy. The majority of Palestinians who live in the West Bank and Gaza are not Israeli citizens, and they do not want to be. They are governed by their own leaders under the PA in the West Bank and the Hamas Party in Gaza.

Furthermore, it bears repeating that no matter where we may now live or have lived before, every Jew is indigenous to the land of Israel including what is now known as the West Bank or Judea and Samaria.

EVIL ISRAELIS: RACISM AND APARTHEID

BDS's false accusations of racism and baseless analogies to apartheid South Africa's segregationist laws trade on the antisemitic libel of the evil Jew.

In my many hours of study on the BDS campaign, I came across a videotaped training seminar for aspiring BDS advocates. The instructors advised the recruits to link the delegitimization of Israel to the moral clarity of the campaign against apartheid

South Africa by mimicking both the tactics *and* the accusations. The campaign against apartheid South Africa, the guides said, was the de facto playbook.

Thankfully, in today's world, racism is reviled, and apartheid, the embodiment of racism, is universally condemned as evil.

"Apartheid," however, refers to a specific set of laws and conditions that existed in South Africa between 1948 and 1994. The closest replication of the South African system in the modern West is the Jim Crow South in the United States before the Civil Rights Movement of the 1950s and '60s. Both apartheid and Jim Crow laws codified the separation of the races, prohibited interracial marriage, and mandated segregated public facilities, including seating on buses and entrances into buildings.

BDS and its boycott supporters would have you believe that these sorts of laws exist in Israel. This is completely untrue. Israel guarantees equal rights to all—regardless of race, religion, ethnicity, or gender—in its founding document, the "Declaration of the Establishment of the State of Israel." The deceitful comparison diminishes the suffering of the Black populations in the US and South Africa and is a cynical exploitation of one group of people to malign another.

After just a few days in the bustling city of Tel Aviv, anyone who visits can see that the charge of apartheid is a lie. Unlike in South Africa or the Jim Crow South, there are no segregated drinking fountains, cafés, supermarkets, bathrooms, hospitals, or schools. There are no backdoor entrances for people of color. Jewish and Palestinian doctors work together and treat all patients regardless of their ethnicity. Jewish and Muslim families play side by side in parks, and Arab and Jewish merchants sell their wares in the same open-air markets. Women in bikinis lie next to women in hijabs on Tel Aviv's silky beaches. Citizens of all ethnicities mingle openly in public arenas, sit side by side in restaurants, and are free to speak their minds and vote their consciences.

All residents of Israel enjoy freedom of religion. In the Old City of Jerusalem, Orthodox Jews hurry down the same narrow cobblestone streets as Catholic pilgrims and Muslim believers. Residents and visitors alike pray in the synagogues, churches, and mosques that are some of the world's most ancient and holy houses of worship.

Israel has guaranteed access to the holy sites to all people, contrary to the prior policies of the Jordanian government, which restricted Jewish access when it controlled the city from 1948 to 1967. Since the reunification of Jerusalem in 1967, freedom of religion and mutual respect and tolerance have flourished.

MURDEROUS ISRAELIS: DISPARITY IN CASUALTIES AND ISRAELIS MURDER PALESTINIAN CIVILIANS

The BDS claim that Israel is intentionally murdering innocent Palestinian women and children, and otherwise showing depraved indifference to human suffering, is classic blood libel. It is present in BDS messaging year-round but gets amplified during every full-scale conflict.

When women and children die in a conflict zone, it is always tragic, and it rightfully tears at the heartstrings of the world. Israel's critics often point to the disparity in casualties between the sides as an indictment of Israel. However, there are many reasons why there are more fatalities among the Palestinians than the Israelis during a given conflict.

Unfortunately, Israel is forced to respond to Hamas, Hezbollah, and other Palestinian groups' attacks coming from populated areas such as Gaza and Lebanon. When that happens, the IDF takes extensive precautions to protect Palestinian noncombatants and uses great restraint.

IDF protocol includes notifying residents of the exact date and time of coming attacks via text message and phone call or by dropping notes from planes flying overhead, giving them time to evacuate. Since 2008, Israel also employs a warning system called "roof knocking," the practice of dropping non-explosive or low-yield devices on the roofs of targeted civilian buildings hiding weapons caches, giving inhabitants time to flee.[194]

Targeting noncombatant civilians is against Israeli military law. Israel's military court investigates any such charges, and soldiers who break the law are punished. Unlike the United States and many other Western nations, the Israeli Supreme Court may review actions of the military and the military court, creating both independent scrutiny and consequences for breaches of this prohibition.

Palestinian militants, on the other hand, bow to no law and use terror and the murder of both Israel's and their own civilian population as a tactic to achieve their political agenda—delegitimatizing the Jewish state. Instead of building bomb shelters and homes, Hamas uses cement and other materials to build underground bunkers to protect combatants and weapons and tunnels to infiltrate Israel.[195] They use women and children as human shields and hide weapons, rocket launchpads, and terrorist leaders among the civilian population, even in hospitals and buildings housing UN and NGO staff and the international press. When missiles are launched from residential or commercial areas, it is impossible for the Israelis to deactivate them without endangering human life.

In addition, Hamas and other Palestinian bad actors often misrepresent the number of innocent civilian casualties by including those of their military combatants.[196] They feed this distorted data to the media, which uncritically parrots the disinformation, typically with no third-party verification.[197] When the rockets fired by Hamas fall short of the border and land in Gaza, the ensuing civilian casualties further inflate the numbers. The result of all this is cries of "war crimes" and "disproportional response" in the press and among the general population.

In 2021, for example, when Israel bombed Hamas headquarters in an Associated Press office building, late night host John Oliver accused Israel of war crimes, saying:[198]

> While Israel insisted that there were military targets in that building and they destroyed it as humanely as possible, even warning people to evacuate it beforehand, for the record, destroying a civilian residence sure seems like a war crime, regardless of whether you send a courtesy heads-up text.

This comment singles out Israel among all nations for rebuke and is beyond ridiculous. When buildings house enemy headquarters or weaponry, they are no longer "civilian residences" and are legitimate military targets.

When a regrettable loss of life occurs in the Palestinian civilian population, despite Israel's efforts to only target military combatants, BDS exploits those deaths to provoke hatred toward Israel in the international court of opinion.

Another, more tragic aspect of the disparity in casualties has to do with a very different attitude between the two sides toward the preservation of life. In Israel, a high value is placed on protecting civilians, both Israel's own and the Palestinians, and in rescuing any injured or captured soldiers.

Israel builds bomb shelters throughout the country, particularly in cities, such as Sderot, Kiryat Shmona, Ma'alot, Nahariya, and Ramat Hagolan, where Israeli residents have fifteen seconds to find shelter after the start of the incoming bomb warning sirens. Israeli homes and commercial buildings are built with safe rooms, and every schoolchild is drilled on safety procedures. These efforts have saved thousands of lives.

By contrast, and regrettably so, the Palestinian terrorists expose the local population to danger and support a culture of martyrdom. Young children are indoctrinated to idealize terrorism and suicide missions. Successful suicide attacks are lionized and the attackers' families compensated for this form of self-annihilation with rewards and monthly stipends.

The false and antisemitic claim that Israel intentionally kills innocent women and children feeds other false claims concerning disproportionate force.

ALL-POWERFUL ISRAELIS: ASYMMETRICAL WAR AND DISPROPORTIONATE FORCE

BDS mischaracterizes Israel's self-defense as "unfair" and the Israeli people as bullies, playing on the trope of the all-powerful Jew.

In BDS propaganda and in many media reports, Israel is cast as Goliath, with its army, and the Palestinians as David, a group of unarmed, untrained civilians. As Goliath, the IDF and the Jewish nation are faulted for participating in an asymmetrical war against the Palestinians and using disproportionate force.

It bears saying that Israel is a very small nation of nine million people that is surrounded by Arab nations on all sides numbering more than one hundred million. These nations have been bent on the destruction of Israel throughout its history and attacked it in several major wars, including those in 1948, 1956, 1967, and 1973. These existential threats have forced Israel to develop a strong military as a necessity.

Many people misunderstand the meaning of an asymmetrical war, believing that it means one side has overwhelming military strength that cannot be defeated (i.e., is all-powerful). In fact, an asymmetrical war only means that each side is using different strategies and tactics against the other. In World War II, the Allies (England, France, and the United States) fought a symmetrical war against the Axis powers (Germany, Japan, and Italy), with both sides using conventional warfare at the time, such as infantry soldiers, machine guns, tanks, and bombs.

However, there have been many asymmetrical wars fought throughout history, and it is not always the larger army or the one with the most modern weaponry that wins. In fact, the term "asymmetrical war" is most often used to explain why established military forces can be defeated by guerrilla forces such as Castro's in Cuba, Mao's in China, the Viet Cong in Vietnam, or even those of the American Continental Army against the British Redcoats in the Revolutionary War—not to mention the probability of future asymmetrical warfare aimed at the West involving cyberattacks and bioweaponry. In an asymmetrical war, each side is fighting by different but deadly means. After all, it was David who won the battle with Goliath.

Palestinian fighters use suicide bombs, knife stabbings, motor vehicles, and other tactics to terrorize Israeli civilians and maximize casualties in the general population. In addition, they are a well-trained fighting force heavily armed with automatic weapons, grenades, suicide vests, and explosives, as well as rocket launchers supplied by Iran via Hezbollah brought in by sea and through illegal tunnels. The range of their rockets has steadily increased over time to the point where they reach major cities, including Tel Aviv. Although Israel's enemies like to portray them as hapless victims, they are, in fact, a formidable enemy.

To listen to Jon Stewart, John Oliver, and others, the all-powerful Israel is waging an "asymmetrical war," and the response of the Israeli military is disproportionate, unjustified, and worthy of denunciation.

John Oliver criticizes Israel for protecting its people and stopping the rocket fire. "There is a massive imbalance when it comes to the two sides' weaponry and capabilities," he said on his *Last Week Tonight* show. When discussing the Iron Dome, which Israel developed, Oliver stated, "While most of the rockets aimed toward Israeli citizens this week were intercepted, Israel's airstrikes were not. They hit their targets."[199]

Israel does what every government is supposed to do—it protects its people with a shield and takes out its enemies' weapons with a sword.

What alternatives do Israelis have? Duck and cover until Hamas runs out of rockets? Let their own people die, so the casualty numbers seem "fairer"?

The children of Gaza are the world's concern, while the children of Sderot, the Israeli town closest to the border, where tens of thousands of missiles have fallen and forced children into underground bunkers, deserve no consideration. The psychological and emotional welfare of these children and their parents, not to mention their physical safety and well-being, are ignored by these Israel Bashers.

Late-night comedy host Jon Stewart even took Israel to task for its life-saving roof-knocking warning system. "What are the Gazans supposed to do?" he asked on an episode of *The Daily Show*. "Evacuate to where? Have you f***ing seen Gaza?! It's this big,"[200] he said, pointing to a map of the region with a tiny Gaza but no other countries delineated, so you could not see how tiny Israel is also.

What are the Palestinians supposed to do? They are supposed to disavow Hamas's pledge to destroy Israel, and as David Horovitz, former Editor of the *Jerusalem Post* and Founding Editor of *The Times of Israel*, suggests, reject its "interpretation of Islam that claims killing Jews, Christians and non-believing Muslims is your guaranteed path to paradise."[201] They are supposed to insist that their leaders use the materials and money they receive to rebuild their lives and protect their citizens. They are supposed to say no to Hamas when it places their families in grave danger by hiding weapons caches in their homes. And if they cannot say no to Hamas because they fear for their lives, they are not supposed to blame Israel when the Israelis fear for their lives and defend themselves.

To characterize Israel as all-powerful is to ignore the real balance of power in the region. Israel has many powerful enemies, including Iran, which seeks to build nuclear weapons with the stated goal of wiping Israel, the "Little Satan," off the face of the map. Iran also supplies its proxies Hezbollah and Hamas with weaponry to attack Israel. In the 2017 hearing before the House Foreign Affairs Committee, Committee Chair Hon. Edward Royce noted that according to one observer, Hezbollah is now more militarily powerful than most North Atlantic Treaty Organization members.[202]

When it comes to Israel protecting itself, it is not about being all-powerful—it is about *"Never Again."*

THE NAZI ISRAELIS: ISRAELIS ARE NAZIS AND COMMITTING GENOCIDE

BDS alleges that the Israelis behave like Nazis and are committing genocide against the Palestinian people.

In a 2021 video blog, Roger Waters refers to the pending eviction of Palestinian Israelis by their Jewish landlords after years of nonpayment of rent as the "genocidal removal of people from their homes."[203] Genocidal? Really? This is not just Nazi inversion but degrades the horrendous suffering and mass murder of millions in real genocides across the globe.

Genocide is the deliberate killing of a large number of people from a particular nation or ethnic group with the aim of destroying that nation or group. As a result of the genocide, the population of that nation or group dramatically decreases. For instance, the genocide in Cambodia in the early 1970s demolished the population by 21–26 percent with the murder of 1.2–1.7 million people. The Rwandan genocide resulted in the murder of five hundred thousand to one million Tutsis and pro-peace Hutus, decreasing the country's total population by as much as 20 percent in 1994. During the Holocaust, the Nazis killed 78 percent of Europe's Jewry, reducing them from 7.3 million to 1.4 million. To date, the Jews have still not recovered from that atrocity. In 1939, the global population of Jewish people worldwide peaked at around 16.6 million. The worldwide population of Jews as of the end of 2019 stood at 14.7 million.[204]

On the other hand, the Palestinian populations in Gaza, the West Bank, and East Jerusalem have grown exponentially, particularly since Israel captured the territories in 1967.

The Jewish Virtual Library addresses the false charge of genocide against Israel as follows:[205]

> While detractors make outrageous claims about Israel committing genocide or ethnic cleansing, the Palestinian population has continued to explode. In Gaza, for example, the population increased from 731,000 in July 1994 to 1,324,991 in 2004, an increase of 81 percent. The growth rate was 3.8 percent, one of the highest in

the world. According to the UN, the total Palestinian population in all the disputed territories (they include Gaza, the West Bank, and East Jerusalem) was 1,006,000 in 1950, 1,094,000 in 1970, and grew to 2,152,000 in 1990. Anthony Cordesman notes the increase "was the result of improvements in income and health services" made by Israel.

Today, over 5.3 million Palestinians live in the West Bank and Gaza.[206] Rather than demolition, the Palestinian people have experienced consistent and even robust growth. This data alone should free Israel of any genocidal allegations.

Despite evidence to the contrary, some people refuse to let Israel off the hook for the charge of genocide arguing that, even if it has not yet succeeded, Israel is *attempting* to commit genocide. Nonsense. Obviously, Israel has the arsenal to decimate Gaza. It chooses not to because of the value it places on human life, including the lives of the people who wish to destroy it. Even during combat, Israel makes every attempt to minimize the loss of innocent Palestinian civilians. In addition to all of the military precautions previously discussed, it allows tons of food, water, and medical equipment and supplies to pass through its borders to aid residents and allows Gazans to enter Israel for medical treatment.[207]

The Holocaust is distinct among other genocides and not just because of its size. Unlike the genocides in the Balkans or Rwanda, for example, the Holocaust was not the outcome of years of feuding or hostility between parties; it was a systematic program of mass murder aimed at exterminating a race of people—the Jews. The Nazis' so-called "Final Solution to the Jewish Problem" was planned at the Wannsee Conference, a high-level Nazi officers meeting on January 20, 1942. The Nazis put pen to paper and planned out the segregation, deportation, and extermination of Europe's entire Jewish population in factory-like death camps.

When BDS and Israel's other critics accuse it of genocide, they are not merely perpetuating an age-old blood libel. They are creating an antisemitic inversion that would have the victims of the world's greatest genocide, the Holocaust, now be falsely cast as perpetrators.

NEXT STEP: KEEP YOUR RESPONSE SIMPLE.

Jews have a right to self-determination in their ancient homeland. Own it.

It is not necessary for you to rebut every single bit of misinformation; you just need to respond to one point and then go on the offense.

For example: accusations of a "land grab" play on the age-old antisemitic trope of "the greedy, thieving Jews" and foment worldwide Jew-hatred.

CHAPTER THIRTEEN

BDS TACTICS

*"If the constant threats, bullying, and slander of Arch Enemy
via email and online does not stop immediately, we will
publish some of the threats we have received from your
supporters, where they claim they will come to some of our
shows and threaten to attack us, both verbally and physically."*

—ANGELA GOSSOW, LEAD SINGER FOR THE
SWEDISH BAND ARCH ENEMY

Never underestimate the intensity of the harassment leveled
against artists who want to perform for their Israeli fans. When
an artist books a trip or concert date in Israel, BDS groups
create a multifaceted campaign to pressure him or her to cancel.
They write statements, petitions, and "open letters" filled with
appalling lies about the Jewish state that become "news" and
often get picked up by mainstream publications. They circulate
memes and Photoshopped images on social media platforms
like Facebook, Twitter, and Instagram associating Israel and
the artist with destruction, racism, apartheid, the murder of
children, and worse.

They repurpose an artist's songs into emotionally evocative videos laden with anti-Israel propaganda. The artist's representatives are often inundated with emails and phone calls. Ads are placed in local and international publications, and protests are staged outside concert halls and inside auditoriums. When an artist cancels a performance for reasons unrelated to the boycott, BDS falsely claims it as a victory in order to create the illusion of success.

STATEMENTS

A BDS campaign often starts with a statement urging the artist to cancel a concert or trip. The statements can come from an individual or a BDS group and can include a list of signatories in the hundreds or, occasionally, thousands. Statements can be generated by grassroots organizations or from entertainment-based groups.

So, for example, when a Canadian artist like Neil Young or Celine Dion is involved, non-entertainment groups like Canadians for Justice and Peace in the Middle East (CJPME)[208] and IJV can be counted on to get involved.

In 2017, a group of more than fifty artists signed a statement calling for Radiohead to cancel its planned performance in Israel. Radiohead had played eight previous concerts in Israel, and it was unlikely the band would be dissuaded. The statement, however, served a secondary purpose: to propagate disinformation and "punish" the band for its disobedience. It stated in part:[209]

> In asking you not to perform in Israel, Palestinians have appealed to you to take one small step to help pressure Israel to end its

violation of basic rights and international law. Surely if making a stand against the politics of division, of discrimination and of hate means anything at all, it means standing against it everywhere—and that has to include what happens to Palestinians every day. Otherwise the rest is, to use your words, "mere rhetoric."

The usual BDS supporters signed on, including Roger Waters, actress Julie Christie, writer/director Mike Leigh, director Ken Loach, musician Thurston Moore, and the band Young Fathers.[210] More importantly, the statement was republished in numerous outlets, including the *Telegraph* and *New Musical Express* (*NME*), a British music, film, and culture website and brand.

Thom Yorke of Radiohead, like many other artists, finds such BDS admonitions and lecturing condescending and arrogant. In a 2017 interview, Yorke told *Rolling Stone*, "It's really upsetting that artists I respect think we are not capable of making a moral decision ourselves after all these years."[211]

BDS takes great care to research each artist's work and his or her philanthropic efforts to tailor the content of its messaging and personalize the statements. The more personal the attack, the easier it is to falsely accuse the artist of hypocrisy and strain the artist's philanthropic relationships. BDS drove a wedge between Scarlett Johansson and the charitable work she did with Oxfam International, as previously mentioned, and sought to do the same with Alicia Keys, Neil Young, British musician Robbie Williams, and the charities they support. The half-truths and outright lies in the statements often give the false appearance of a well-researched document. In addition, BDS has a go-to roster of artists it can rely on to support most campaigns, giving the appearance of muscle and raising the visibility of the statement.

Prior to 2011, BDS statements were typically released in pro-BDS, anti-Israel online publications such as the *Electronic Intifada* (a Palestinian web publication founded by Ali Abunimah) and *Mondoweiss* (journalist Philip Weiss's antizionist blog) and then occasionally picked up by a few mainstream media outlets.

Today, by contrast, statements often first appear in traditional publications—such as the left-leaning *The Guardian*, a popular English newspaper known for its extensive arts coverage—giving them greater credibility.

OPEN LETTERS

An "open letter" is a personal letter to the artist that is published for the world to see. Oftentimes, they initially appear on APUK's website as well as other anti-Israel BDS blogs or smaller publications before getting picked up by mainstream media, where the letter is exploited to attract readers.

An open letter is an instrument of pressure disguised as a personal plea. These "letters" often come from activists who are not celebrities, and they tend to be more personal in nature than group statements. The writer will relate his or her backstory and experiences, giving the note a human face. Sometimes, organizations will write what they call a letter since it is addressed to a specific artist, but if it has a long list of signatories, I categorize that as a statement.

An open letter from two female New Zealand activists, one Jewish and one of Palestinian descent, addressed to New Zealand songstress Lorde was published in a local newspaper and then posted on social media. It praised Lorde's progressive ideals and said that playing in Israel would be hypocritical, but the letter's power lay in its simple and personal tone. In part, it read:[212]

> Our names are Justine and Nadia. Justine is part of Dayenu...The driving principle of Dayenu is saying "enough" to Israel's crimes against Palestinians...Nadia is a Palestinian New Zealander. Her family live[s] under occupation in the West Bank.

The post caught the eye of the young singer, who responded online before ultimately canceling her concert date, "Noted! Been speaking w many people about this and considering all options. Thank u for educating me i am learning all the time too."[213]

Concert promoter Eran Arielli, who suffered significant financial loss from Lorde's cancellation, only had kind words for the young performer:[214]

> I have no complaints about her, and beyond that, my opinion of her has not changed one millimeter...The truth is that I was naive to think that an artist of her age can withstand the pressure involved in coming to Israel, and I take full responsibility and ask the forgiveness of fans, admirers, and other dreamers.

There are not very many American artists who are avid boycott activists. An exception is Alice Walker, the Pulitzer Prize–winning author of *The Color Purple*, who, as mentioned, famously refused to allow her book to be translated into Hebrew and wrote an open letter to Alicia Keys in 2013 falsely comparing Israel to apartheid South Africa and the Jim Crow South. "It would grieve me to know you are putting yourself in danger (soul danger) by performing in an apartheid country that is being boycotted by many global conscious artists," she wrote, referring to Keys as a "beloved daughter and friend."[215]

Walker's letter was picked up by BET.com, the preeminent multimedia conglomerate targeting African American audiences with a reach of more than 88 million households. Ben Silverman, Emmy- and Golden Globe–winning executive producer of *The Office, Jane the Virgin,* and *Ugly Betty,* wrote a rebuttal to the misinformation in a counterpoint opinion. In it, Silverman praised Israel's democracy and diversity and congratulated Ms. Keys on her message of love to a region continuously looking for peace.

Despite pressure from Walker, Waters, and BDS groups, Keys refused to give in. "I look forward to my first visit to Israel," she told the *New York Times.* "Music is a universal language that is meant to unify audiences in peace and love, and that is the spirit of our show."[216] Keys extended her stay for five days after her performance to experience Israel for herself. Since then, she has brought Palestinian and Israeli musicians together, most famously in a televised Central Park concert with Israeli singer Idan Raichel and Palestinian qanun virtuoso Ali Amr, in the spirit of "unity, love, compassion, and forgiveness."[217]

Despite Keys's decision not to cancel, and Silverman's strong response, I believe Walker's statement remained influential to an audience that holds her in high esteem.

Private letters from high profile individuals can also have an impact. Before their return performance in Israel, revered Brazilian musicians Gilberto Gil and Caetano Veloso were visited by two Brazilian BDS supporters who hand-delivered letters from Desmond Tutu and Waters. They ended up canceling the tour.

PETITIONS

Another favorite BDS tactic is petitions. A delegation of Palestinian Americans delivered a petition with more than twelve thousand signatures to the Board of Directors of Alicia Keys's Keep a Child Alive, a nonprofit organization close to her heart, falsely claiming that Israel abuses and tortures children.

The signatures on these petitions, however, are difficult for third parties to monitor or verify, so it is certainly possible that the same people are signing the petition under different names and accounts to exponentially inflate the numbers.

In addition, the same individuals are likely to sign separate petitions addressed to different artists. Accordingly, 2,700 signatories to petition "A" and 5,000 signatories to petition "B" do not necessarily add up to 7,700 different BDS supporters.

In 2018, a petition targeting American songstress Lana Del Rey and the Meteor Festival launched jointly by PACBI and JVP gathered nearly fifteen thousand signatures and spawned the Twitter hashtag #LanaDontGo.[218] Unlike Keys, however, who kept her 2014 concert date and spent five days in the country getting to know its people, Del Rey canceled her scheduled performance shortly before the festival.

LETTER-WRITING CAMPAIGNS

When there is enough time, groups will also launch letter-writing campaigns. Petitions are intended to make artists afraid that they are alienating their fanbase, while the primary function of letter-writing campaigns is to overwhelm the artist's representatives. Public relations representatives are required to make their clients aware of offers and communications.

Concert promoter Guy Beser of Bluestone Entertainment reported that Jon Bon Jovi told him in 2019 that "he's received more than 5,000 letters from BDS activists who are against the show but he said, 'I chose Israel and I'm coming, no one will cancel my show.'" According to Beser, "This is an example of an old school artist that isn't afraid about his career."[219]

Although these mini manifestos are typically tweaked to resonate with an individual artist, they all demonize Israel. Statements, open letters, petitions, and letter-writing campaigns always follow the same blueprint: "If you care about [fill in a social issue close to the artist's heart—e.g., the downtrodden, apartheid, children, the environment, clean water], do not perform in Israel."

In all the years I have dedicated to this mission, I have never seen a BDS statement, petition, or letter that provided any semblance of balance, called for reconciliation, or asked an artist to make a positive contribution to better the lives of the Palestinians. I have never seen a statement, petition, or letter that asked an artist to contribute funds for musical instruments, give a free concert in Ramallah, provide mentorship, teach, or support peace by backing an Israeli–Palestinian collaboration in the arts.

Support for peace typically comes from entertainers who refuse to boycott the Jewish homeland. Music legend Leonard Cohen donated proceeds from a 2009 Tel Aviv concert to organizations working for peace. Ian Anderson, lead singer of the rock band Jethro Tull, donated earnings from three separate concert tours to charities, including the Polyphony Foundation, which brings together Arab and Jewish children for the study and performance of classical music.

Statements are also written in support of Israel or against the boycott. When I was director of the Creative Community for Peace, we issued several statements signed by our board of directors and members of our Professional Network Committee that were picked up by international publications and circulated worldwide.

Individuals who speak out against the boycott via group statements are not usually attacked personally (i.e., there is safety in numbers), which is part of the rationale behind group statements, but there are exceptions.

One of those exceptions is J. K. Rowling, a non-Jew who has stood up against the cultural boycott of Israel and against antisemitism.[220] As previously discussed, the author of the *Harry Potter* books joined an anti-boycott group of 150 writers, artists, and media personalities called Culture for Coexistence.[221] In 2015, they issued a statement in *The Guardian* that read in part:[222]

> Cultural boycotts singling out Israel are divisive and discriminatory, and will not further peace. Open dialogue and interaction promote greater understanding and mutual acceptance, and it is through such understanding and acceptance that movement can be made towards a resolution of the conflict.

Rowling, however, faced an avalanche of criticism alone. Her Twitter feed was blanketed by posts comparing Israel to the "Death Eaters" in the *Harry Potter* series and the author herself to Potter's archenemy, Voldemort. Some BDS supporters said that "Harry would be disappointed" and that their childhoods had been ruined because of her stance. PACBI issued a statement, and Mia Oudeh, a twenty-five-year-old Palestinian music teacher, published an angry open letter on her Facebook page scoffing at the notion of reconciliation:[223]

> No cultural engagement between Palestinians and Israelis will ever build bridges, because rather than the "two sides are to blame" argument the letter you signed endorses, there are no two sides... To the Palestinians, many of whom rely on *Harry Potter* as a means of inspiration and escapism, you have outed yourself as a sympathiser of today's present-day Nazis who are conducting ethnic cleansing as we speak.

Oudeh's open letter went viral. The fallout was so intense that Rowling felt obliged to respond but refused to back down, saying that the artists "are voices I'd like to hear amplified, not silenced" and that a cultural boycott "places immovable barriers between artists and academics who want to talk to each other, understand each other and work side-by-side for peace." Rowling also said, however, that she deplored most of Israeli prime minister Netanyahu's actions. "The Palestinian community has suffered untold injustice and brutality," she wrote. "I want to see the Israeli government held to account for that injustice and brutality."[224]

This offended many Israelis, who felt that she was giving a pass to Palestinian terrorism and relentless incitement and placed sole responsibility for the conflict on Israel. More open letters followed, including some from Israeli supporters, and more social media wars. The British author was caught in the crossfire but remained resolute that Israel should not be subjected to a boycott. Since then, she has denounced antisemitism within the British Labour Party. *Lethal White*, the fourth book in Rowling's Cormoran Strike mystery series, written under the pen name Robert Galbraith, includes an antizionist villain.

CALLS AND EMAILS

While they are in the crosshairs, artists often feel isolated and overwhelmed. That goes for their representatives as well. I once got a call from the agent of an iconic movie star. His client was scheduled to accept an award from a North American organization affiliated with a university in Israel. He told me he was being inundated by phone calls and a constant flow of emails demanding that his client decline the award.

The agent then made the mistake of responding to a phone call by the executive director of a prominent BDS organization. He thought, he said, that if he made her feel heard and explained that he shared many of her criticisms of Israel, it would diffuse the situation. It did not, and he was now overwhelmed by what he had unintentionally invited in. He said if he had known what was going to happen, he would have advised his client not to accept the award in the first place.

Unfortunately, there was not much I could do to stop this kind of harassment since it was only days away from the scheduled event when the agent contacted me. But I assured him that the abuse would stop shortly, and they would move on to another victim.

Not only did the movie star accept the award, but I was delighted to see that a few years later, this superstar took his first trip to Israel.

REPURPOSED SONGS

BDS will also create propaganda videos that play an artist's popular songs over Photoshopped images associating both the artist and Israelis with human suffering. Fragmented video clips from uncited sources are combined to tell a biased account of the Palestinian narrative. In 2013, prior to Alicia Keys's July 4 performance in Israel, BDS proponents created a video using Ms. Keys's recording of "Girl on Fire" over Photoshopped images of soldiers and what appeared to be Palestinian women in snapshots of altercations without context.

Using the song "Rockin' in the Free World," BDS proponents intercut clips of Neil Young's performances with still images and videos depicting war scenes, large building equipment, and a concrete wall (to reiterate: only about 5 percent of the security barrier is concrete) among other charged visuals to insinuate that if he performed in Israel, he was supporting an apartheid state and therefore not "Rockin' in the Free World."

BDS will also rework the lyrics and rerecord a song inside a video. For example, just days before she was scheduled to perform, Ms. Lauryn Hill dropped out of a Tel Aviv concert as the result of a heated social media campaign that included a video based on her cover version of "Killing Me Softly."

The video contained images of destruction from unknown locations and superimposed a clearly Photoshopped image of what we were supposed to believe were Palestinian women standing on rubble. By associating the artist with these images of war and violence, the makers of the video were implicitly questioning her humanity. The story of the cancellation was picked up by *The Guardian*, the *Daily Telegraph*, and *Ynet*, along with music publications *ContactMusic.com* and *Fader*.

BDS makes these videos without the artist's permission, so they can be taken down for copyright infringement. However, they are an effective means of grabbing the attention of the artists and their fans, and by the time they are taken down, much of the damage has already been done.

PROTESTS AND DEMONSTRATIONS

In addition to media campaigns, BDS proponents organize protests and demonstrations outside the artist's concerts along the route to Israel. Aussie musician Nick Cave was hit hard by protests organized outside concert halls along his tour in Amsterdam, Berlin, Antwerp, Paris, Copenhagen, Nottingham, Glasgow, and London.

BDS proponents create dedicated Facebook pages where they share graphics, talking points, and event details. The protests themselves tend to be small, but they accomplish two important things: their signs and chants disseminate disinformation outside venues to hundreds of concert goers and add pressure on artists by making them feel hunted.

Protests take place inside events as well. Radiohead faced boos, chanting, and Palestinian flags at the Glastonbury Festival in England, where they were headlining prior to their Israel tour in 2017.

Gil Scott-Heron, a sixty-one-year-old American jazz legend, was similarly hounded in 2010, a year before his death. He was heckled and his concerts were disrupted. Security had to be called and audience members threatened with removal. Finally, after disruptions during a performance at London's Royal Festival Hall days before he was headed for the Holy Land, Scott-Heron reluctantly announced he would not be going ahead with his Israel tour date.[225]

ADVERTISEMENTS

Both BDS proponents and Israel supporters will sometimes raise funds for advertisements in mainstream newspapers. When the subject revolves around the cultural boycott, the go-to publications are either industry-based media or the *Los Angeles Times* (the de facto neighborhood paper for the movie capital of the world) and the *New York Times*. A full-page ad is an excellent way to draw attention to your cause, attracting many more eyeballs than an article or an op-ed.

In 2016, the Academy Award "swag bag" included a trip to Israel. It is common knowledge within the industry that Oscar nominees receive swag bags filled with expensive gifts that include items like electronic devices, beauty treatments, and first-class trips. Other countries such as Japan have also given trips to nominees in the past without raising eyebrows. In 2016, however, two high-profile BDS organizations, US Campaign to End the Israeli Occupation (End the Occupation) and JVP, used it as an opportunity to trash Israel. They placed an ad in the *Los Angeles Times* pressuring Academy Award nominees, including film stars Matt Damon, Cate Blanchett, Jennifer Lawrence, and

Christian Bale, to refuse the gift, implying that the artists were being bought off.

On the other side, in 2014, I helped circulate a statement[226] (detailed in a later chapter) in support of Israel and ultimately signed by more than three hundred high-level Hollywood executives and entertainers, including Arnold Schwarzenegger, Sylvester Stallone, and Kelsey Grammer, and placed advertisements featuring that statement in *Variety,* the *Hollywood Reporter,* the *Los Angeles Times,* and the *New York Times.* The story was picked up by more than eighty publications worldwide.

Rabbi Shmuley Boteach and media mogul Haim Saban, both fierce Israel supporters, have also been known to place ads in defense of Israel and critical of Israel Bashers.

FALSE CLAIMS OF VICTORY

Musicians cancel concerts in Israel for a variety of reasons, just like they do everywhere. BDS propagandists, however, typically misrepresent any cancellation in the Jewish homeland as support for the boycott and a victory for their cause.

BDS proponents make false claims of victory to create the illusion they are succeeding at their campaign, there is momentum, and their movement is growing. They will publicly thank the artist and post happy, self-congratulatory messages on social media. These false tales of success appear in anti-Israel publications and then get picked up by mainstream media. Then, in a classic example of triangulation, other mainstream media reference the first mainstream publication, perpetuating the misinformation ad infinitum, and thus false reports are validated to the public.

As in other countries, cancellations in Israel can occur due to scheduling conflicts, security issues, lack of ticket sales, or personal reasons. Carlos Santana, the Pixies, and the Beach Boys all canceled for their own reasons but were labeled boycott supporters—when, in fact, they happily performed a few years later, belying the earlier reports.

Other times, when concert dates are announced prematurely and the parties fail to reach an agreement, no concert date is ever set. Amazingly, BDS proponents still view this as a victory and will take a bow.

In 2019, Colombian singer Shakira—whose father is Lebanese—was in conversations with Live Nation Productions for an Israeli concert as part of a summer tour that included Turkey and Lebanon. A local Israeli publication incorrectly reported that the deal had been finalized, and BDS supporters in Lebanon wrote to Shakira asking her to cancel her "date." Although the deal had never been consummated and the promoters posted on Twitter that the announcement was incorrect, BDS supporters took to social media to celebrate their "victory."

Other times, typically reliable publications will repeat rumors of boycott support with no basis for such speculation. I remember one incident where an entertainment industry publication reported that a very popular American band refused to perform in Israel. I knew otherwise, so I contacted the journalist and directed him/her to a video clip in which the lead singer said he/she could not wait to play in Israel. Despite evidence to the contrary, the writer was adamant that he/she had good sources and refused to make a correction. Since then, the band has rocked crowds in Tel Aviv twice, and the publication has never made a correction.

Artists are sometimes forced to cancel appearances in Israel for safety reasons. Since its inception, Israel has had to engage in numerous defensive wars, which at times makes the country unsafe for visitors and citizens alike. During such times, a concert promoter or the Israeli government cannot guarantee the safety of the performers or the concertgoers, so concerts must be canceled or postponed.

When Canadian Neil Young had to cancel a Tel Aviv concert for security reasons during the 2014 Israel–Gaza conflict known as Operation Protective Edge, the BDS Facebook page "Neil Young, Tell Me Why You Would Play for Apartheid Israel" spun Young's cancellation as a political victory: "We appreciate Neil Young for refraining from entertaining apartheid Israel."[227] BDS is at its cynical worst when it celebrates such cancellations as victories.

In addition to ongoing conflicts, many artists worry about terrorist attacks. Concert promoter Daniel Ben Av, who has brought the likes of Katy Perry, Ed Sheeran, and Sting to Asian markets like China and Japan, worked in the Israel concert scene in the mid-1960s. Israelis were as passionate about their music then as they are today, filling thirty thousand seats for artists they loved, like folk singers Pete Seeger and Odetta. Ben Av often had to reassure artists that life was peaceful and safe there. I too have had to explain the realities on the ground to jittery managers, agents, and lawyers. When the crew of one high-profile rapper became concerned about skirmishes on the Gaza border, I sent the rep a map of the country so he could see the long distance between the clash and Tel Aviv. When artists are looking for reassurance, Keren Urinov of Live Nation Israel, a premiere concert production company, sends contemporaneous photos of life in Tel Aviv—the beaches, cafés, markets—to settle nerves.

When an artist cancels for safety reasons, it is not a BDS win. Frequently, he or she will rebook when things feel calmer. Promoter Ben Av told me that, before his death in 2016, René Angélil, Celine Dion's husband and manager, declined to bring her to Israel for safety reasons. In 2020, four years after his death, the superstar singer booked a date in the Holy Land as part of her *Courage* tour, which was canceled due to the pandemic. She rescheduled for June 2021[228] but had to cancel once against due to COVID-19 restrictions.

In November 2015, while the American band Eagles of Death Metal were performing at the Bataclan in Paris, the audience was attacked by terrorists wielding automatic rifles, grenades, and suicide vests. In 2017, a terrorist killed twenty-two children and wounded a hundred more in a bombing at an Ariana Grande concert in Manchester, England.[229] Thankfully, there has never been a terrorist attack at a concert in the Holy Land.

ATTACKS ON MIDDLE EASTERN AND ARAB ISRAELI ARTISTS

Arab and Muslim artists from other Middle Eastern countries also face enormous pressure to boycott Israel. Arab Israeli artists are often coerced into what is sometimes referred to as a "noncooperation boycott" that prevents them from collaborating with their Jewish peers or presenting Israel in a positive light. When these artists dare to reach out to their Israeli brethren in a gesture of peace and reconciliation, they face vicious backlash and worse from their own communities.

In 2020, for example, Noamane Chaari, a Tunisian music producer, released the song "Peace between Neighbors," performed by Israeli singer Ziv Yehezkel. Chaari faced immediate internal backlash, received death threats on social media, and said he was fired from his job at a state broadcaster.[230]

In 2017, Miss Iraq, Sarah Idan, took a selfie with Miss Israel at the Miss Universe contest and posted it on social media. In a one-on-one interview, the Iraqi beauty told me she immediately received calls from Iraqi officials threatening her with treason, jail, and revocation of her citizenship. Her parents received death threats and had to leave the country within three days. She was forced to make a statement saying, "I don't support Israeli policies in the Middle East, and I support the Palestinian cause."[231] She is not allowed to return to her native country and now lives in Los Angeles.

* * *

Although you, the reader, may find BDS tactics repugnant, you may also feel removed. After all, you might think, I am not an artist or an Israeli or even a Jew.

To see the cultural boycott campaign solely as an artist or Israeli problem, however, is to be looking into the wrong end of the binoculars. The risk posed goes far beyond Israel's borders. It is an attack on audiences everywhere.

People want to make their own decisions about what music they hear and which films they see. Even those among us clamoring for "safe spaces" do not want strangers editing our iTunes playlists.

The cultural boycott campaign politicizes art and eviscerates the role of artists as peace ambassadors and agents of change. The fight to counter its efforts is a battle to liberate art.

NEXT STEP: KNOW YOU MAKE A DIFFERENCE.

Assume the artist is a good person and that he or she cares about Jew-hatred.

Write a supportive open letter to an artist who is under fire. Open letters are personal and reflect not just facts but your personal feelings and experiences. Speak from your heart. Post it on social media, tag me, and send it to your local newspaper.

Remember the New Zealand girls who wrote that open letter to Lorde made huge waves. You can too.

CHAPTER FOURTEEN

CELEBRITIES MAKE NEWS

*"You can also chalk it up to the CNN syndrome—if
your knowledge of someplace only comes from
media reports, then it's going to be a very skewed
image. After the first time I came, I realized that my
impression of Israel was completely inaccurate."*

—STEVE WILSON, ENGLISH MUSICIAN

The cultural boycott campaign tactic is to attack artists and accuse them of supporting the human rights violations it falsely accuses Israel of committing. Its strategy is to use the newsworthiness of these attacks on artists to draw attention to its lies and prejudice hundreds of millions of people across the globe.

College divestment campaigns and pickets outside of Trader Joe's do not have the same pizzazz as a celebrity in the crosshairs of a political battle. Stories about rock icons under BDS siege will garner the attention of international mainstream media, including radio and TV broadcasters. Reports in industry-related publications, like *Variety*, *Hollywood Reporter*, *Billboard*, and *Rolling Stone*, reach entertainers and color their perceptions of the realities in the region.

Whether an artist succumbs to the pressure and cancels is secondary to its newsworthiness; it is the campaign itself that captures the imagination. BDS open letters, petitions, and protests leading up to a concert get covered with enormous zeal, so failed campaigns often receive the same coverage as successful ones. Even when outlets attempt to be evenhanded, they invariably recap BDS's stated goals and repeat its malicious allegations. Wide coverage of cancellation stories creates the misconception that the boycott is far more successful than it is.

The relationship is mutually beneficial. BDS gets a platform to spread its lies, and news outlets get stories with "star power." This has given BDS an outsized microphone and the ear of the world.

THE ROLLING STONES—ISRAEL 2014

The media coverage of the Rolling Stones's June 4, 2014 performance in Israel and the BDS campaign led by Roger Waters and Nick Mason—the English drummer best known as a founding member of Pink Floyd—is an excellent case study of this phenomena.

More than a month before the concert date, Waters and Mason wrote an open letter to Mick and the gang on Salon.com saying in part, "Playing Israel now is the moral equivalent of playing Sun City at the height of South African apartheid."[232] Other publications reported on and quoted from the letter, including the *New York Daily News*,[233] the *Washington Post*, CBSnews. com, Yahoo!, the *Independent*, the *New York Post*, ArabNews. com, *Mother Jones*, *Mashable*, the *Press-Enterprise*, *The Forward*, and *The Sydney Morning Herald*.[234] To give you an idea of the reach of this story: *The Sydney Morning Herald* is an Australian daily newspaper distributed nationally with a print and online readership, as of September 2019, of 2,394,000—almost 10 percent of the total population of Australia.

BDS talking points continue to be disseminated even when the cultural boycott campaign fails miserably. The Stones played HaYarkon Park as scheduled, and the concert and visit were by all accounts a smashing success. The band visited historic and religious sites, spoke a bit of Hebrew to the audience, and respectfully started their concert forty-five minutes late to give those celebrating the Jewish holiday Shavuot extra time to get there.

The day after, however, *CBS This Morning* gave short shrift to the enormous success of the concert. In a segment titled "Battle of the Bands: Stones Ignore Plea by Pink Floyd to Skip Israel," reporter Anthony Mason uncritically promoted Waters's campaign to the program's three million viewers. He featured a video clip from Pink Floyd's "Another Brick in the Wall" and an excerpt of Waters's anti-Israel diatribe at the UN.

The segment did not include a single comment from anyone opposing the boycott or supporting Israel. Further minimizing the colossal failure of the Waters/Mason effort, host Gayle King added, "They drew attention to the cause. They wanted to do that. But the Stones say, you know, we don't want to disappoint the fans."[235]

The morning show take was repeated on CBSNews.com in an article entitled, "Sour Note: Rolling Stones Perform in Israel, to the Chagrin of Pink Floyd,"[236] widening its audience. BDS fans were delighted with the slant.[237]

Glaring TV segment titles and news headlines like those above highlight the controversy and reinforce the BDS message that Israel is a pariah state. Segment titles on TV news programs are critically important. They set the stage for the viewer or reader, creating an expectation that is often self-fulfilling even if the news story itself is more nuanced (which it was not in the coverage by CBS). In a newspaper or magazine publication, the title and subtitle of the story have even more impact, given the average reader's propensity to read headlines and skim through stories. In both cases, headlines and titles are what turn up in Google searches and on media feeds. A misleading title does a great deal of damage.

Titles are also not-so-subtle tells of the media outlet's bias. Imagine if CBS This Morning had entitled the Stones/Waters segment, "Attack on Cultural Exchange Fails: Stones Ignore Pressure by Pink Floyd to Skip Israel." Or if CBSNews.com had titled its story, "On a Happy Note: Stones Israel Concert Major Success, Despite Seeming Harassment by Pink Floyd's Waters."

When reporting on one celebrity brouhaha, news publications often reference other brouhahas that emphasize the controversy around playing in Israel. On the same day as the CBS This Morning show, the Daily Mail, a popular British tabloid, featured numerous pictures of the British rockers during their sightseeing tours of Jerusalem and Israel with relatively positive captions. However, the paper also highlighted a firestorm ignited a few days before when American singer Justin Timberlake posted a photo of himself praying at the Western Wall with the caption "The Holy Land…What an experience. I will never forget this day. #Israel."[238]

The negative tenor in the *Daily Mail* was compounded by quoting heavily from the Waters/Mason open letter and giving ample space to the PA's religious affairs minister Mahmoud al-Habash, who was quoted as saying, "There will not be peace without Jerusalem as the capital of Palestine."[239]

Some publications do succeed at impartiality and accuracy. Even though it included information about the movement's stated motives and claims, the *Washington Post* reported on the Waters/Mason attack on the Stones evenhandedly, referencing Israel's popularity as a destination for international musicians. William Booth and Ruth Eglash wrote:[240]

> The Stones's decision to ignore Roger Waters and Nick Mason of Pink Floyd underscored Israel's growing popularity as a stop for major musical acts, and it signaled a setback for a campaign known as [B]oycott, [D]ivestment and [S]anctions (BDS).

The *New York Daily News* quoted from Waters and Mason's letter but noted that "Detractors have called Waters an antisemite for his crusade against Israel—a charge the British singer vehemently denies, despite having regularly compared the predominantly Jewish country to Nazi Germany." And it also added that "Alicia Keys, Elton John, Lady Gaga, Rihanna[,] and Madonna are among the artists who've ignored Waters's picket line in recent years."[241]

Stories about celebrities have extended shelf lives. Six days later, people were still talking about the Stones event. On June 10, *New York Times* columnist Roger Cohen wrote an opinion piece for the Gray Lady referencing the Waters/Mason letter and campaign. The newsman supported Jagger's decision to play Tel Aviv and protested Waters's previous comparisons of Israel and Germany's Nazi regime. "BDS can too easily be commandeered by anti-Semites posing as antizionists who channel the quest for peace in a direction that ultimately dooms Israel as a national home for Jews."[242]

This gave Roger Waters the opportunity to jump back on the soapbox and into the limelight with a letter to the editor calling the reference to antisemitism a smoke screen.

It is important to note that, in this case, the dustup was one-sided. The Stones never responded directly or indirectly to Waters and Mason either before or after the concert other than by keeping the concert date. Yet, the story made big news reaching many millions of people.

Balanced reporting is good and appropriate but not common enough. Hundreds of artists perform in Israel every year, and in almost every instance, BDS proponents call for them to cancel their performances, generating endless fodder for international publications.

MUSIC MEDIA ADVOCATES FOR BDS

Certain media outlets go beyond mere biased reporting and are seemingly corralled by their progressive ideology into helping to do BDS's job for them. This is even more troublesome when those outlets are industry-based because they can influence a cross-section of artists and art and music fans. *Rolling Stone* magazine and *Pitchfork,* for example, appear to be on the BDS team, seemingly disseminating its messaging, misrepresenting facts, and piling on to artists who disagree with the campaign.

Rolling Stone has been promoting BDS on its pages since at least 2013, when it published Roger Waters's claim that the Israeli government was "running a similar regime" to South Africa during apartheid and his call to fellow artists to boycott the Jewish homeland.[243] It consistently repeats the former Pink Floyd bassist's often-disturbing comments, such as telling Bon Jovi, "You stand shoulder to shoulder with the settler who burned the baby," without questioning, much less verifying, the claims. And it fails to confront Waters on his blatantly antisemitic remarks, such as his claim that the Jews control the media.[244]

In a 2019 story about Grammy-winner Demi Lovato's trip to Israel with their mother, the magazine, in its exuberance to bash Israel, besmirched the singer, who was recovering from drug addiction and mental health issues, to advance an antisemitic trope about Jews and money. It insinuated that Lovato was paid by the Israeli government for their trip there (they were not) and that the source of the funds was somehow suspicious.* [245]

The magazine seems to go out of its way to ignore the real news story in lieu of disseminating BDS talking points, as evidenced in its coverage of the 2019 Eurovision Song Contest hosted in Israel. Eurovision, held annually since 1956 (except for 2020,

---

* In 2021 Demi Lovato announced they are non-binary and prefers they/them pronouns. Sophie Lewis, "Demi Lovato Announces They are Non-Binary and Changing Their Pronouns," CBS News, May 19, 2021, https://www.cbsnews.com/news/demi-lovato-non-binary-pronouns-podcast-announcement/.

due to the COVID-19 pandemic), ranks among the world's most watched non-sporting events every year, with hundreds of millions of viewers globally.

In the lead-up to the event, BDS proponents petitioned the Eurovision organization not to hold their event in Israel. They asked participating nations not to attend. They pleaded with companies not to broadcast the contest and stations not to carry the show. And of course, they pressured international artists to cancel.[246]

Singers from forty-one countries took part in the contest. Not a single artist canceled. BDS's efforts to thwart the event were a complete failure. That was the news story.

Rolling Stone's coverage, however, focused on BDS's talking points. It quoted PACBI, which called the Jewish state criminal and Madonna's participation as a guest performer "'immoral' at a time when Palestinians are being brutally oppressed."[247] Further, the music publication claimed the contest was "at a time when fewer and fewer major artists are performing in apartheid Tel Aviv."[248] The latter claim was all the more ironic considering the overwhelming participation in the Eurovision contest and the large number of major artists who had performed in Israel in the preceding years.

Perhaps *Rolling Stone* believes that its support of the cultural boycott makes it look hip and reflects its counterculture values. What it does, in my view, is demonstrate its lack of true journalistic standards.

Pitchfork, an online American music magazine based in Chicago and owned by Condé Nast, has consistently adopted a similar stance. The site is a division of Pitchfork Media, which organizes a popular music festival each summer in the Windy City.

In 2017, *Pitchfork* reported on the open letter from artists Roger Waters, Thurston Moore, and others urging Radiohead to "think again" about performing in Israel and quoted Moore, who said that a canceled gig is "a small sacrifice in respect to those who struggle in honorable opposition to state-sponsored fascism."[249] Not so much sharing a news story as it was helping to spread disinformation and solicit adherents, the article created the illusion of a wave of support for a cultural boycott by artists— referring to "countless" artists—and provided a convenient link to APUK's website.

Subtitled, "Please do what artists did in South Africa's era of oppression: stay away, until apartheid is over," the article quoted extensively from the open letter but failed to provide balance or any semblance of a counterargument to its charges.[250]

Pitchfork did not tell its readers about the hundreds of artists who visit or perform in Israel every year and who speak glowingly about the Jewish state, despite the harassment they receive from the likes of Roger Waters and (mostly ill-intended) grassroots groups. It conveniently neglected to mention even a handful of the high-profile artists who have rejected the call to boycott, including Justin Bieber, Justin Timberlake, Jon Bon Jovi, Claire Danes, Helen Mirren, Rihanna, Alicia Keys, Pitbull, Lady Gaga, Neil Young, Ricky Martin, Joss Stone, Carlos Santana, Red Hot Chili Peppers, Quentin Tarantino, Paul McCartney, the Rolling Stones, Seal, Kevin Costner, Cyndi Lauper, Yanni, DJ Tiësto, Moby, and Bob Dylan, to name a few.

Pitchfork, which bills itself as "the most trusted voice in music," did not balance the negative comments by musician Thurston Moore with even a smattering of positive descriptions, such as the one by Jay Leno, who describes Israel as "the only democracy in the Middle East" and "this one little paradise in the Middle East where freedom reigns."[251] Not to mention Paul McCartney and others who kept their concert dates in Israel despite threats to their physical safety from BDS and its supporters.

Publications such as *Rolling Stone* and *Pitchfork* would do well to look before they leap into bed with those who, in the opinion of many, seek to silence artists to impose their political will on artists and audiences alike.

NEXT STEP: COMPLAIN.

Write letters to the editors of newspapers and magazines when they disseminate Jew-hatred disguised as a news event.

Write an op-ed on the subject. Small local papers are just as important as bigger ones.

CHAPTER FIFTEEN

SOCIAL MEDIA

"The boycott is an anti-peace movement."
—MICHAEL DOUGLAS, AMERICAN ACTOR

For BDS, social media is both a tactic and a strategy. It is a tool to pressure artists, but its primary function is to disseminate anti-Israel and antisemitic propaganda. Social media gives BDS the ability to reach a different audience than mainstream media and connect with otherwise untapped demographics. (Its demographics skew younger and less knowledgeable.)[252]

According to a 2020 Pew Research Center report:[253]

> The rise of social media has changed the information landscape in myriad ways, including the manner in which many Americans keep up with current events. In fact, social media is now among the most common pathways where people—particularly young adults—get their political news.

The report goes on to say that individuals who rely on social media for their news have greater exposure to conspiracy theories (e.g., that "powerful people" intentionally planned the COVID-19 pandemic), lower levels of knowledge about major current events, and are less concerned about being fed made-up news.[254]

Thus, social media helps create the perfect storm for BDS. Here, BDS can attack artists on social media platforms and spread disinformation about Israel in easy-to-remember sound bites that can be mindlessly parroted. Deceptive slogans like "Apartheid Israel" and "Free Palestine" are as powerful as they are misleading. Photoshopped images link Israelis to suffering children and poison hearts and minds around the world. Dangerous conspiracy theories about all-powerful and evil Jews and Israelis thrive on social media.

The collective fanbase of artists and celebrities is enormous, and by tapping into the social media reach of these individuals, BDS can reach billions of people. As of the time of this writing, the top eleven artists on Facebook have almost a billion collective followers.[255] And that is just eleven people on one social media platform.

GOOD REVIEWS AND BAD BACKLASH

Almost all artists, entertainers, and celebrities who have visited Israel or have worked successfully with Israeli companies speak glowingly of the experience in their follow-up interviews and social media posts.

Many, like Demi Lovato, Kathie Lee Gifford, and Madonna (who has called Israel "the center of the world") are moved by its spirituality. Others, like actor Ashton Kutcher and U2's Bono, admire its technological developments, and others still, like Lady Gaga and Claire Danes, love the vibrant nightlife.

When artists visit Israel, they are free to move about as they please and speak to whomever they want. Visits can be, and have been, arranged to cities in the West Bank. The artists' positive comments in interviews and posts are based on their personal experiences. While it is obvious that no one can predict what an artist might say while there or upon their return (witness the relentless criticism from Roger Waters since his 2006 concert), Israel supporters are optimistic about the outcome, while BDS proponents appear to be profoundly worried (or else why try to stop artists from going there?).

The good reviews by celebrities who have visited, however, are dwarfed by the negative blowback they receive from BDS proponents. If the artist responds, it becomes more fuel for the fire, typically igniting a hailstorm of mudslinging between BDS and Israel supporters. The controversy always benefits BDS because it makes Israel appear controversial—a place of hostility and conflict rather than the home of nine million diverse citizens living in relative peace.

It does not take much to set off the social media attacks. In fact, most often it is not a political comment but simply a positive statement about Israel that lights the fire.

In 2011, an Israeli fan asked pop star and daughter of evangelical Christians Katy Perry to "Please pray with us."

She wrote back that she was: "I am! My prayers are for you guys tonight, SHALOM!!"[256] Happy Israelis expressed appreciation, but BDS drowned out the positive messages with a flood of condemnation.

Here are just a few of the hateful and threatening personal posts that were visible to Perry's 109 million followers:[257]

> "Katy Perry is praying for Israel. Wait, what? Aren't they killing Palestinian babies at this moment? Yes."

> "I do not understand how come there're Arab fans for @KatyPerry or other celebrities who are pro Israel! SHAME ON YOU. #PrayForGaza."

> "LISTEN PERI PERI, you better be praying that Israel leave Palestine ALONE."

> "You heartless lesbian, Israel has killed THOUSANDS of PALESTINIANS. Yet you're gonna pray for Israel? You shiz."

> "So @katyperry is praying for Israel. Does she look like the kinda girl that prays?"

> "I used to luv @KatyPerry. Shocked to find out she was supporting #israel."

> "Nice, @KatyPerry prays for Israel that spits on #Gaza and its murdered children like little 2 year old Malik killed by a bomb with his dad."

> "I hope your private jet crash lands in Palestine so they can stamp on you like the wh*** you are see if Israel come help you."

> "Go to hell with ISRAEL b*****."

In less than a day, the singer seemed overwhelmed and running for cover when she tweeted, "A kid asked me to pray for him & I did. I don't support ANY side of violence in ANY place for ANY reason. #peaceinthemiddleeast #sheneutral!"[258] Artists are the only targets of these intimidating social media assaults. The attacks also warn the artists' fans about what could happen to anyone who supports Israelis.

During her 2019 trip to Israel, Demi Lovato posted photos of their baptism in the Jordan River and spoke about the positive impact it had on their life. They wrote:[259]

> I am an American singer. I was raised Christian and have Jewish ancestors. When I was offered an amazing opportunity to visit the places I'd read about in the Bible growing up, I said yes…This trip has been so important for my well-being, my heart, and my soul. I'm grateful for the memories made and the opportunity to be able to fill the God-sized hole in my heart. Thank you for having me, Israel.

The post got more than 3.5 million likes and 770 comments.

BDS supporters (who are so concerned about human suffering), however, thought nothing about attacking a fragile young person with comments like the ones thrown at Katy Perry. Lovato was obviously no match for their predators, and you can see them gradually crumbling under the pummeling in their responses below:[260]

> *"Okay but do y'all realize, I don't have an opinion on middle eastern conflicts nor is it my place to have one being an American singer and you're asking me to choose one?"*

"That's literally asking me to choose a side. I will not choose a side. I went to a place, for religious purposes, THAT'S IT."

"Well clearly I can't win with you unless I do what YOU want me to, so idk what to tell you."

And then:[261]

"Oh don't worry, you guys made me feel terrible about it, and prob will continue to do so. I'll be hibernating."

Beaten into submission, Lovato posted a follow-up comment implying that they were somehow duped: "I accepted a free trip to Israel in exchange for a few posts. No one told me there would be anything wrong with going or that I could possibly be offending anyone. With that being said, I'm sorry if I've hurt or offended anyone, that was not my intention."[262] Many Israel supporters felt betrayed by the implication that Lovato had been deceived.

It is disappointing that Lovato did not take responsibility for their decision to go. Despite their denial, it seems to me that the singer may have in fact been informed of the possible consequences of going. They are represented by Scooter Braun (manager), best known for discovering Justin Bieber, and Braun is fully aware of the BDS campaign. Even if they were informed, however, it appears they may not have been emotionally prepared for it. Many Israelis backed off their initial criticism and feelings of betrayal out of empathy. Nonetheless, BDS won a significant round.

Social media can also have more tangible consequences for

the artists. In 2019, Jennifer Lopez booked dates in Russia, Turkey, Spain, Israel, and Egypt as part of her *It's My Party* tour—a worldwide celebration marking her fiftieth birthday. Lopez received massive pressure to cancel the Tel Aviv leg but refused. Both Lopez and then-fiancé Alex Rodriquez, former third baseman for the New York Yankees, visited Israeli sites and documented the visit on social media. Rodriguez posted a photo of the couple at the Mount of Olives to Twitter with the caption "Jerusalem, you are unforgettable. What a perfect finale to our first trip to this beautiful land."[263] When Jennifer Lopez wrote, "Tel Aviv was incredible"[264] on her Instagram feed after her concert and the post was shared by her and Rodriguez, more than 93 million of their followers on Instagram had a chance to see it. The backlash came in the form of ticket sales. Only two thousand people attended her next stop in Cairo—a far cry from her usual fifty to sixty thousand attendees.

NEARLY EVERY CONCERT ANNOUNCEMENT CREATES A SOCIAL MEDIA STORM

After announcing her participation in the Israel Meteor Festival in 2018, sultry American singer Lana Del Rey initially responded to social media attacks by saying the performance was not a political statement. She tweeted:[265]

> What I can tell you is I believe music is universal and should be used to bring us together…My plan was for it to be done w a loving energy w a thematic emphasis on peace.

And:

> I would like to remind you that performing in Tel Aviv is not a

political statement or a commitment to the politics there just as singing here in California doesn't mean my views are in alignment w my current governments opinions or sometimes inhuman actions.

Then, as the pressure mounted, the singer's resolve began to deteriorate. A few days later, according to *Vulture,* the culture and entertainment site from *New York* magazine, she attempted to appease her attackers by announcing that she would add a performance in the West Bank to her tour.[266]

It is extremely difficult to add a new location to a tour on such short notice, which, to my mind, made the offer empty to begin with. Not surprisingly, shortly thereafter, Del Rey announced her "postponement" of the Meteor Festival on Twitter, saying her show was being delayed "until a time when I can schedule visits for both my Israeli and Palestinian fans."[267]

It is not an unfamiliar pattern. An artist books a concert date in Israel and gets falsely accused of murdering Palestinian babies. At first, they defend their decision, but some, as it appears to be with Lana Del Rey, ultimately cannot handle the heat and cancel their tours.

Many Israelis felt the incident was a publicity stunt. The festival promoters added these choice words to the announcement of her cancellation on their website: "We do appreciate her for choosing [M]eteor to help her score some press attention."[268]

The relationship between social media and digital/traditional media is fluid and mutually reinforcing for BDS. Mainstream media publishes stories about the social media frays of celebrities, which serves to further spread the lies.

The story of the Lana Del Rey furor was carried in numerous entertainment publications, including *Billboard*,[269] *Pitchfork*,[270] *Vulture*, and *Deadline*,[271] as well as mainstream media.

ATTACKS HERE, THERE, AND EVERYWHERE

Even a rumor about an artist going to Israel or a "hello" can spark social media attacks. In 2016, a Springsteen fan briefly met the legendary singer-songwriter and told him she had just flown in from Israel. He responded, "I really need to play there."[272] From that, rumors circulated about a Bruce Springsteen and the E Street Band concert in Israel, and band members Steven Van Zandt, Garry Tallent, and even the Boss himself received social media jabs.

When Billie Eilish dropped her second album, *Happier Than Ever*, she made short promotional videos targeting different markets. The one she made for her Israeli fans began with "Hi Israel," and as David Lange of *IsraellyCool* reported, was met with outrage.[273] "It's occupied Palestinian land not Israel," one Twitter user snapped, while another threatened, "We'll gonna unfollow you bc you deserve it, educate yourself and see what israel are doing for Palestine children."[274]

In addition to attacks on the artists' pages, BDS will also barrage artists' social sites, including their fan pages and YouTube videos. For example, the campaign targeting Neil Young made its way onto a fan website called Thrasher's Wheat, polluting the image of Israel for thousands of his devotees.[275]

A 1993 YouTube video of Michael Jackson performing in Israel was forced to close its comments section. The besieged administrator said:[276]

> I've been forced to close the comment section due to the shameful behaviour of someone who use[s] this video to do political remarks. This is MUSIC. Nothing else. You can share your opinion of Israel, Palestine, [etc. etc. on another] kind of video. Not this one.

These BDS campaigns, like other social media campaigns today, have been accused of using bots to goose up their impact. Bots are applications that perform automated tasks like reposting comments and making them appear as if they come from unique users. That was certainly the case in 2014 when Alicia Keys saw hundreds of posts on her platforms from supposed Ethiopian Israelis claiming they were second-class citizens. Some have claimed that many of the social media attacks on Lovato mentioned earlier were also the result of bots.

MEMES

In addition, social media communicates on a more visual and visceral level, often using graphic images called "memes" to pack an emotional punch.

Memes typically combine photos of the artist with Photoshopped images of Israel's purported crimes against humanity (the photos sometimes taken from other war-torn regions). These images draw heavily on classic antisemitic tropes associating Israel with murder, war, and cruelty while endlessly repeating the unfounded charge of apartheid. The intent is not to make the artists or their fans think but to make them respond emotionally.

Each meme combines a plea for the artist to boycott with an implied threat to his or her career and reputation.

Some of these inflammatory images include:

- A meme pairs the Bon Jovi band with an image of a fighter jet (presumably Israeli) dropping bombs.
- Taylor Swift is Photoshopped standing atop a building reduced to rubble while playing her guitar, oblivious to the ruin around her.
- Scarlett Johansson is painted with a scarlet letter "A," for apartheid, on her forehead.
- Canadian American folk-rock singer-songwriter Martha Wainwright is coupled with pleading children and marred by a bloody Jewish star.

HOW ARTISTS RESPOND TO SOCIAL MEDIA ASSAULTS

The response to BDS attacks differs from artist to artist. Not all artists monitor their social media feeds. Some artists are even blissfully unaware of the attacks, particularly if the messaging is confined to social media. On more than one occasion, I have contacted an artist's representative to see how they were responding to some lies posted on their feed only to discover they were unaware of them. When this happens, it does not mean the posts are less impactful on the artist's fans.

Although it is hard to generalize, I have noticed that musicians in different genres react differently to attacks. For example, jazz is very popular in Israel, so there are numerous bookings throughout the year and several major jazz festivals annually. These musicians tend to be more sensitive and reactive to the criticism, which is not surprising given the intimate relationship they have with their audiences.

Heavy metal musicians and punk rock bands, on the other hand, can be more defiant.

John Lydon, a.k.a. Johnny Rotten of the Sex Pistols, for example, has been quoted as saying:[277]

> If Elvis-f******-Costello wants to pull out of a gig in Israel because he's suddenly got this compassion for Palestinians then good on him. But I have absolutely one rule, right? Until I see an Arab country, a Muslim country, with a democracy, I won't understand how anyone can have a problem with how they're treated.

Another punk rocker's agent told me his client enjoyed the fray. Punks Against Apartheid, co-founded by Alexander Billet, a music journalist and frequent *Electronic Intifada* blogger (the *Electronic Intifada* is an antizionism website), came on the scene in 2011, attracting little interest.

Younger artists tend to be more sensitive to social media conversations in general. Most have been active users all their lives, as have all their friends. They have experienced firsthand the power and importance of this medium. Young artists like Lorde and Demi Lovato, who have weathered fewer life storms, are more likely to fold under pressure.

BDS singles out minority artists, implying that if they do not support the boycott, they are betraying their community. It claims that artists who perform for their Israeli fans are giving a "stamp of approval" to the false claims of Israeli colonialism, apartheid, oppression, and ethnic cleansing. BDS supporters highlight the erroneous charge of Israeli apartheid to members of the Black and people-of-color artist communities, believing it resonates more strongly with them.

Israel haters are aggressively reaching out to a young and urban market through hip-hop music. According to Brandon Gaille, a popular marketing blogger who has appeared in publications such as *Forbes,* "hip hop...has the youngest audience demographic in the world today...Almost two-thirds of the hip-hop audience is between the ages of 18–34." It also has a large Hispanic audience, with more than 70 percent of Hispanic adults saying they are hip-hop listeners.[278] What better way to reach them than through the cultural boycott campaign?

Although many artists do not view or personally post on their social media platforms, some do—regardless of how large their following. Rihanna's Twitter post "#FreePalestine" and Katy Perry's tweet "I pray for Israel" were both posted by the artists themselves. Kim Kardashian has developed relationships with fans on social media by answering their tweets and occasionally meeting them in person. You can judge for yourself from the social media excerpts in this book whether you think the posts are authentic.

Typically, when I am asked by artists' representatives how to respond to the noise on social media, I tell them that every artist must chart his or her own course, but responding will only encourage more attacks, not quell them. When the anti-

Israel Code Pink organization applied pressure on Lionel Richie regarding his planned September 2019 concert, he blocked their Twitter account.

I recommend that artists mute BDS on social media and make a public statement against the campaign and in support of the artist's role in building cultural bridges of peace.

NEXT STEP: DO NOT LET BDS CONTROL THE NARRATIVE.

Go on the offense. You do not win wars by exclusively playing defense.

It only takes a few good men and women to make a difference. Be one of them.

CHAPTER SIXTEEN

ISRAELI ARTISTS FACE DISCRIMINATION

"Shoot the Jew!"

—SOUTH AFRICAN BDS PROTESTERS TO ISRAELI JAZZ ARTIST

The pressure on international artists to shun Israel is only one side of the cultural boycott coin. BDS also wants to prevent Jewish Israeli artists from performing or exhibiting outside Israel.

BDS hounds international venues to rescind invitations, humiliates Israeli artists, and intimidates audiences. There are calls for cancellations and disrupted performances, and of course, there is always the threat of physical violence.

In 2015, while visiting London, I was excited to discover that the Jerusalem Quartet was performing at St. John's Smith Square. The award-winning Jerusalem Quartet is one of the most talented and in-demand string quartets of its generation and brings joy to thousands of music lovers across the globe.

Although I knew that prior performances had been disrupted by hecklers and I was not surprised to see protesters outside (there were only fifteen or so of them gathered on the sidewalk right at the entrance), I was not prepared for how unsafe and threatened they made me feel.

Protesters greeted patrons with vitriolic chants, drums, and inflammatory anti-Israel banners. Audience members were forced to scurry past as the protesters yelled and shoved flyers at us. "Shame on you!" they shouted, "Music cannot hide the ugly reality of Israeli apartheid!"

In the auditorium, the quartet lifted my spirits, but I could not ignore the ugly chants that seeped through the walls during quiet interludes, such as "One, two, three, four—Occupation no more! Five, six, seven, eight—Israel is a terrorist state!"

At the intermission, my friend and I went outside and saw that the situation had escalated. Protesters were calling for Israel's destruction, chanting, "From the river to the sea, Palestine will be free!" Others were now having heated face-to-face arguments with people on the street. The London police were there to break up the disturbance, warning the protesters that under the UK's stringent laws, they could be reported for a hate crime.

The next day, the *Evening Standard*'s Nick Kimberley devoted almost a third of his review to the protests, expressing his political sympathies in a music critique. "I duly felt pangs of liberal guilt," Kimberley wrote, "and…a modicum of anxiety."[279] Naturally, he ignored the attempt to censor artists and the brazen expression of modern-day antisemitism.

Liberate Art was also at the scene of a 2018 demonstration in New York City organized by Adalah-NY against the Israeli dance troupe Batsheva where roughly fifty protesters showed up chanting, "Dancers have to take a stand, no excuse for stealing land."[280] Broadwayworld.com called the intimidation "a vibrant, musical protest on the sidewalk."[281]

The world-acclaimed Israeli Philharmonic Orchestra (IPO) is a frequent victim of international protests. The IPO was formed by Jews escaping Nazi Germany in the 1930s.[282] In 2011, the BBC's broadcast of the Proms concert at London's Royal Albert Hall was interrupted twice by protesters organized by the PSC. Igor Toronyi-Lalic, the Arts Editor of the *Spectator* and Director of the London Contemporary Music Festival, who was in attendance, gave a more accurate depiction of the experience when he said that the shouting created the atmosphere "of a riot."[283]

The 2018 performance of the IPO in Morocco was not publicized beforehand to protect the IPO members from harm.[284]

In 2013, when Israeli jazz artist Daniel Zamir performed in South Africa (SA) at Wits University in Johannesburg, intimidation escalated into death threats. BDS's charade of peaceful political action was exposed when the cry "Shoot the Jew!" rang out on campus like the shouts of a lynch mob.[285] Other inflammatory cries included, "there is no such thing as Israel" and "Israel apartheid."

According to *The Jerusalem Post*, BDS coordinator Muhammed

Desai appeared to defend the call to shoot Jews telling a student newspaper that the word "Jews" was not meant in a literal fashion.[286]

Local Jewish leader Mary Kluk replied in a statement: "What this incident unmistakably shows is that BDS-SA's real agenda is not to stand up for the Palestinian cause but to incite hatred, and possibly even violence, against Jewish South Africans."[287]

In 2018, a Norwegian gender-identity festival blocked six Israeli choreographers from participating on political grounds, claiming Israel's presence would "whitewash or justify its occupation of the Palestinian people."[288]

The shunned artists responded in a letter in which they asked the Norwegian festival organizers:[289]

> Would you reject a Spanish artist for the Spanish policy against Caledonia and the Basques? Would you reject a Saudi artist for Saudi restrictions on women's rights? Would you reject an American artist for the American policies regarding the "Muslim ban" regulations? Would you reject a Syrian artist for bloodshed caused by the Syrian government? Would you reject an Iranian artist for the forceful reaction to the last uprising in the country? If we were Muslim Arab Israeli artists, Christian Arab Israeli artists, Bedouin-Israeli artists, Circassian-Israeli artists, Druze-Israeli artists, or Jewish-Israeli artists living abroad, would we have been denied participation in your festival as well?

Shamefully, the organizers neither responded nor changed their position.

In 2020, top Israeli model Arbel Kynan arrived in Paris to be photographed by a very reputable fashion company as part of Haute Couture Fashion Week. Working the Haute Couture runway is a prestigious job in the modeling world, and she said that the photo shoot went "very well." During casual conversations with the other models, however, she let it be known that she was Israeli. As the model shared with her thirty thousand followers on Instagram, a few days later, her agent told her that a Lebanese designer did not want her to take part in the show, and she had been dropped. There were four Lebanese designers in the event, and the culprit was never identified or reprimanded.[290]

The boycott campaign takes its greatest toll on Israeli artists in the fine and performing arts. A case in point is the anti-Israeli artist protests and exclusions at the Scottish Edinburgh Fringe Festival (the Fringe)—the largest performing arts festival in the world, attracting hundreds of thousands of visitors every August.

Protests at the Fringe are usually organized by the anti-Israel Scottish Palestine Solidarity Campaign (SPSC) and date back to at least 1997 but have been growing steadily in their impact.

In 2014, Edinburgh's Underbelly Theater, which participates in the festival, was forced to cancel a performance of an Israeli rap opera, *The City,* performed by the Israeli Incubator Theater acting troupe, after anti-Israel demonstrators gathered outside the venue, disrupting nearby events at some fifteen other venues. The protesters cursed at the actors and called them baby killers, creating such a disturbance that extraordinary security measures were needed, but no additional funds were available. The performers said they would sing in the streets if they had to, and they did. No other Fringe venue offered to host them.

In 2015, there were no Israeli state–sponsored performances at the Fringe. The comedy *5 Kilo Sugar* had to get private funding from two Jewish charities, the Andrew Balint Charitable Trust and the Shoresh Charitable Trust.

BDS's alleged justification for discrimination against Israeli artists is that Israeli cultural institutions like IPO, Batsheva, and Habima, as well as some individual artists and art projects, receive partial financial aid from the government. BDS groups argue that if an event organizer or concert hall welcomes these artists, they are endorsing, or "art washing," the policies of the Israeli government. BDS says that showcasing Israeli artists makes Israel look good, as if that is some sort of crime. Every government that helps export its country's arts does so for two primary reasons: to support its artist community and to enhance its image in the world. This litmus test—"You cannot perform here if we do not like the policies of your government"—is not imposed on artists from any other country.

Israeli art is not a handmaiden to government policy even when it does receive funding from the ministry. In fact, very little of Israeli art is political in nature, and when it is, like most political commentary in open, liberal democracies, it tends to be critical of the government. When the Incubator Theatre troupe was shut down at the Fringe, its artistic director, Arik Eshet, responded:[291]

> We are not agents of the government of Israel. Yes, we do receive funds from [the government], although only in the last two years.

We started in pubs making satire and it was usually at the expense of the establishment, and we get support from [the government] even though we are not politically correct.

The Incubator also receives funding from the Beracha Foundation, which promotes Arab–Israeli cooperation, and Eshet was a former board member of Waah-at i sal-amm/Ne-ve shal-om, a community school established by Jewish and Palestinian citizens of Israel. The troupe has never been a surrogate for the policies of the government.

If its goal is to change certain policies of the Israeli government to benefit Palestinians, as opposed to destroying the Jewish nature of the state, BDS would embrace Jewish Israeli artists who support their point of view, but it does not. BDS supporters regularly turn their backs on Jewish Israeli artists, even when those artists sympathize with their cause or are activists for peace.

The composer, music producer, and ardent BDS advocate Brian Eno denied permission for Ohad Naharin, Batsheva's choreographer and artistic director, to continue using his music for a series of performances in Italy after Eno discovered that the Israeli embassy was sponsoring the event. In a statement, Batsheva responded:[292]

We have fully respected Mr. Eno's wish and replaced the music in Ohad Naharin's piece Humus from "Three"—and with great sadness—as we believe that this kind of action is useless and has no contribution towards solving the conflict, ending the occupation[,] or bringing peace to our region. Ohad Naharin has been a political activist for years within Israel, and never hesitated to be very vocal about the situation in the West Bank and the conse-quences of the occupation. His deep commitment to the freedom of the human spirit is reflected in his actions as well as artistic creations.

In 2017, BDS pressured the Lincoln Center to cancel its sched-uled performances of David Grossman's anti-war play *To the End of the Land* by the Habima National Theatre and the Cameri Theatre of Tel Aviv. Grossman's son Uri, a tank commander in the IDF, was killed in action in the 2006 Lebanon War. The play is about a mother who tries to escape from her worry over her son's military service by going on a hike in the Galilee. The book upon which it was based has been described as one of the great anti-war novels of our time.[293]

BDS casts Israel's support for the arts as strictly self-serving when, in fact, it is a gift to the world. Creative collaborations between Israeli and Palestinian artists help build bridges. The Israeli government, to its great credit, often helps fund co-ventures, even when they are critical of the government, such as the documentary *5 Broken Cameras*, a first-person account by a West Bank Palestinian of protests in a village affected by the security barrier. The film *Paradise Now*, about two Palestinian men preparing for a suicide attack in Israel, was directed by Israeli Palestinian Hany Abu-Assad and produced by Israeli Jewish producer Amir Harel. The Israel Film Fund underwrote the film's distribution in Israel.[294]

Israel's support of its artists and cultural organizations is not tied to the artists' politics. Israeli Academy Award nominees *Waltz with Bashir* and *Beaufort* are both films critical of the Israeli government.

Government support of the arts is roundly applauded when it comes to other countries. A hallmark of open, liberal societies is that they support their artists without censoring them, and such support should be applauded, not shunned.

The artist community in the United States has long recognized the importance of the government-funded National Endowment for the Arts (NEA). At the beginning of the Trump administration in 2016, many feared that the NEA might be eliminated in the new US federal budget. Members of the arts community voiced their opposition in national publications across the country. Not one artist lobbied for defunding the program because they disagreed with the policies of the newly elected administration. They championed fiscal support for the arts as essential to cultural exchange and a lynchpin of democracy. They linked government sponsorship to the future of freedom of artistic expression.

BDS claims it is targeting the Israeli government, but it is the Israeli artists who suffer. Thousands of artists across the globe receive government funding from their country to participate in international events, yet only Israeli artists are singled out for discrimination because a political crusade does not approve of certain policies of their government. "Every group that comes to the Fringe from other countries is unable to come without government help," according to the Incubator's Eshet.[295]

In addition, BDS has forced the exclusion of Jewish Israeli artists even when they have not received government funds. Israeli filmmaker Roy Zafrani's independently financed documentary *The Other Dreamers*, about disabled children pursuing their dreams, was rejected by a film festival in Oslo because it was not critical of Israel's treatment of the Palestinian people. Festival organizers there openly embraced the cultural boycott, declaring they would only exhibit films from Israeli filmmakers if the films focus on the "illegal occupation" or "the blockade of Gaza." To leave no doubt that they would filter based on not just the country of origin and subject matter but point of view, the organizers added the qualifier, "or [films that are] otherwise about the discrimination of Palestinians."[296]

The antizionism messaging spread by BDS has led some legitimate, nonpartisan NGOs to go to ridiculous lengths to single out and condemn art and entertainment from the Jewish homeland. In December 2021, for example, the Twitter feed of the International Committee of the Red Cross (ICRC) said it was keeping an eye on the hit Israeli television series *Fauda* because it contained scenes that depicted violations of international humanitarian law.

"Like many of you, this year we've also watched @FaudaOfficial and noted a number of violations of #IHL," the account posted, using an acronym for "international humanitarian law."[297] A thread of tweets followed in which the ICRC called out scenes of torture and hostage-taking from various episodes of the Netflix show, which follows a fictitious undercover counterterrorism unit in the IDF.

"Hiking in the forest is good for you. Taking hostages is illegal in any circumstances, and specifically prohibited by #IHL," the Red Cross smirked, using the Israeli show as a model of bad behavior.[298]

Bear in mind that this is a fictional show, as in make-believe.

Also bear in mind that the organization has no concern about similar violations that appear in thousands of American and international feature films and television shows, including *24*, *The Americans*, *The Bridge*, *Killing Eve*, and *Homeland*.

Taking a page out of George Orwell's *1984*, the Red Cross then invited its followers to squeal on the showrunners, adding, "Check out this Twitter thread and tell us if you see more!"[299] With all of the human rights violations going on across the globe, this international human rights organization is deeply concerned about the behavior depicted in a fictional television series? This would be laughable if it were not such deeply disturbing proof that once again, Israel is being singled out and villainized.

Placing obstacles in front of artists that discourage or inhibit their right to perform based on their nationality is discrimination and creates a chilling effect on freedom of artistic expression for all. There is a distinction between boycotting an artist because you do not like his or her politics versus boycotting an artist because you do not like his or her country's politics, or the politics of a country the artist performs in. Artists are clearly responsible for their own actions and clearly not responsible for the action of governments, which, in some cases, they passionately denounce. Singling out Israeli artists for a litmus test not imposed on artists from any other country is to me cultural apartheid and antisemitic.

If lack of government funding for the arts erodes freedom of artistic expression and cultural exchange, then surely cultural boycotts do far more so. Cultural boycotts beget cultural boycotts. Artists who support cultural boycotts can be targeted themselves. BDS seems to be appealing to left-leaning artists with an antisemitic "ends justified the means" argument—i.e., it is okay to support censorship if it leads to the delegitimization of Israel.

Martin Luther King, Jr. dreamed that his children would one day be judged not by the color of their skin but by the content of their character. Perhaps if he were alive now, he would dream of the day that Israeli artists would be judged not by the cover of their passport but by their contributions to the world.

NEXT STEP: SUPPORT ISRAELI ARTISTS WHEN THEY TOUR.

Buy tickets for shows. Post about your positive experiences on social media.

Follow me on social media to see which international venues are being pressured to rescind invitations to Israeli artists. Retweet and share my posts. Write letters and sign petitions.

CHAPTER SEVENTEEN

ARTISTS WHO SUPPORT ISRAEL

"We can call [my relationship with Israel] a love affair."
—MARIAH CAREY, AMERICAN SINGER

Many people I speak with in my professional capacity express dismay at what they see as a lack of entertainment-industry support for Israel and a failure by entertainers to condemn the boycott campaign. Their perception, however, is not correct. Although their comments and actions do not get the same coverage as disparaging remarks against Israel (and do not seem to linger in the public consciousness as long), artists do support Israel and speak out against BDS.

SPEAKING UP

One artist who never fails to raise his voice for the Jewish homeland is eight-time Grammy-winner Ziggy Marley. In 2015, Liberate Art brought Marley together with the JNF in celebration of the JNF clean water initiative. The musician was honored for his philanthropic work and charitable contributions, helping to provide clean, safe drinking water to people in developing nations. Liberate Art recorded a video of Marley's acceptance speech and his heartfelt expression of love for Israel, where he said he and his late father "feel a very spiritual and personal connection to that land and the people of that land."[300] The video went viral.

Academy Award–winning actor and producer Michael Douglas brought attention to the resurgence of antisemitism in a 2015 *Los Angeles Times* op-ed, where he described "an irrational and misplaced hatred of Israel"[301] as a source of modern-day Jew-hatred. In 2020, Douglas joined then-chairman of the Jewish Agency for Israel Natan Sharansky on a tour of college campuses as part of a campaign to counter the antisemitism and the BDS movement that exists in our universities.

A legend in the world of entertainment, Jay Leno has always been a friend to Israel and has said, "I'm a huge supporter of Israel and always have been. It is a democracy in the Middle East and I don't like to see the little guy getting picked on by the big guy."[302]

He finds the perception of Israel as a bully to be ridiculous. "I don't understand how Israel is the bad guy here," says Leno, "It doesn't make any sense to me."[303] The comic legend is clear on where he stands: "At some point in your life, you have to sort of take sides. I tend to side with the Jewish point of view on many things...I realize how important Israel is."[304]

Late-night talk show host Conan O'Brien might not regard himself as a champion for Israel, but an episode he did, "Conan Without Borders: Israel," presented the best case against antizionism by showing the Israeli people as they truly are.

Approximately twice a year, Conan would take his show out internationally and shoot a special in a different part of the world. In 2017, Conan wandered the streets, beaches, and cafés of Tel Aviv and Jerusalem and randomly interviewed the people he met. Whether engaging a hunky young Israeli, experiencing a mud bath in the Dead Sea, or having an impromptu coffee in the living room of a stall owner in Jerusalem's souk, the show and the people were warm, charming, and eminently likeable.

Oscar-winner Helen Mirren has been to Israel several times and has been a vocal critic of BDS propagandists. Her relationship with Israel began in 1967 when she volunteered on a kibbutz, and she fondly recalls picking grapes and doing kitchen duty: "I am a believer in Israel…I think this is an extraordinary country filled with very, very extraordinary people," she said in a 2016 interview. On getting to know Israel, she said, "It's just a lucky… accident in my life that I have had this privilege."[305]

Mirren has played two strong-willed Jewish women in her storied career: a Mossad agent who is assigned to track down a feared Nazi war criminal in *The Debt* and an elderly Jewish refugee who fights the Austrian government to reclaim a Gustav Klimt painting stolen from her family by the Nazis in *Woman in Gold*. In 2021, she signed on to portray Israel's iconic prime minister Golda Meir in the feature biopic *Golda* with Israeli director Guy Nattiv. The Oscar-, Tony-, and four-time-Emmy-award winner adamantly opposes the cultural boycott campaign: "The artists of the country are the people you need to communicate with and make a relationship with and learn from and build upon. So, I absolutely don't believe in the boycott."[306]

Similarly, musician Alan Parsons never fails to speak out against the campaign, whether it is in a radio or TV interview or as a member of a Liberate Art anti-BDS celebrity panel where he said, "BDS is an appeal for a boycott, not a boycott. As long as it is an appeal, it can be rejected."[307] That panel also featured actor Mark Pellegrino, entertainment attorney Ken Hertz (whose firm represents major Hollywood stars), Israeli bass player Guy Erez, and iconic writer/producer/director David Zucker (the man behind *Airplane!* and the *Naked Gun* franchise).

Unabashed, Pellegrino has gone on Twitter to defend Israel's right to protect itself, saying, "The alternatives for the Israelis are to fight or be destroyed. This is a choice FORCED upon them by the terrorist."[308]

Mayim Bialik, American actress and star of *The Big Bang Theory* television series, is an observant Jew and single mother who also holds a doctorate in neuroscience. A self-described "proud Zionist and a proud liberal," she is outspoken about how she feels about Israel:[309]

> I'm very grateful for the opportunity to be alive and to be able to speak freely about my love for this country which my grandparents prayed for as they fled Eastern Europe, and to hopefully educate people through my public platform about the truth about Zionism and Jews and the State of Israel.

Her support for Israel has led to antisemitic attacks on social media and calls to boycott her and her shows. "It hasn't yet, that I know of, impacted my acting career, but it has impacted the way that I am seen, and that does impact my career in terms of speaking engagements and endorsements." True to her beliefs, she has said, "I'm happy to take that public bullet for the state."[310]

Bill Maher is a popular American comedian and political commentator. Maher was particularly brilliant in the August 16, 2019, episode of *Real Time* when he asked his guest panel, "Is BDS fair?" and "Does Israel deserve this?"

Maher questioned the morality of the BDS campaign, including its antisemitic motives and its lack of context and historical perspective. Pointing to the Jewish victims of ethnic cleansing in Arab and Middle Eastern countries like Morocco, Tunisia, Egypt, Iraq, Eritrea, and Iran that are never spoken about, he asked the group, "Why doesn't anyone mention that in the media? It's not exactly a one-way street here, is it?"

When the panel dithered, Maher answered his own question saying, "BDS is a b******* purity test to make people look woke who actually slept through history class."[311]

Bill Maher has also pointed out that Israel is being held to a standard no other country has ever been held to. "It's a war that Hamas started and somehow when Israel reacts to this, they have to do it in some way that doesn't kill any civilians... If the situation were reversed, Hamas would kill every single person in Israel."[312]

American singer and actress Vanessa Williams visited Israel in July 2014, in the middle of the conflict with Hamas dubbed Operation Protective Edge. Undeterred by the rockets shot into Israel, she visited its beautiful historic and modern sites and posted photos and rave reviews all over social media. Kathie Lee Gifford, former *Today* cohost, published a book about Israel, cowritten with a rabbi. In 2016, she marched as honorary marshal in New York's "Celebrate Israel Parade."

In 2014, along with other members of the entertainment industry, including attorneys Patti Felker, Fred Toczek, and Marty Singer and agent Michael Kives,[313] I circulated a statement in support of Israel's right to defend itself, saying in part, "Hamas cannot be allowed to rain rockets on Israeli cities, nor can it be allowed to hold its own people hostage."[314]

Ultimately, more than three hundred key members of the industry lent their names to this important statement, including artists and entertainers such as Arnold Schwarzenegger, Sylvester Stallone, Bill Maher, Seth Rogen, Kelsey Grammer, Tom Arnold, Minnie Driver, Sarah Silverman, Eriq La Salle, Josh Malina, Benji Madden, and Joel Madden.

Signatories also included Hollywood legends, such as film and music producers Lou Adler and Ivan Reitman and TV and film writer/director Aaron Sorkin, and Hollywood power brokers, including the heads of the major agencies.[315]

During the eleven-day Hamas–Israel conflict in 2021, American actress Debra Messing took to Instagram and Twitter, saying, "There are 22 Muslim countries, there is 1 Jewish state. It is the only place Jews are safe. Hamas is the cause of the violence. Israel must defend itself."[316]

CCFP also issued a press release calling on members of the entertainment community to stop posting misinformation and one-sided narratives that only work to inflame the conflict instead of bringing about peace. Signatories included Kiss frontman Gene Simmons, singer Michael Bublé, actress Selma Blair, and American reggae rapper, beatboxer, and artist Matisyahu.

I could go on, but I think E Street Band member and *Sopranos* actor Steven Van Zandt summed up the feelings of many artists when he ended a Twitter battle with this remark: "You and the other Israel boycotters are politically ignorant obnoxious idiots. Israel is one of our two friends in the Middle East."[317]

SHOWING UP

Actions speak louder than words, and artists demonstrate their opposition to this unwarranted condemnation of Israel, first and foremost, by continuing to go there. A few artists cancel their Israeli performances in response to BDS pressure, but their numbers are incredibly small. In 2012, for example, there were more than two hundred artists scheduled to perform in Israel, and in 2013, there were nearly three hundred. Of those, 95 percent kept their scheduled appearances despite the barrage of attacks on their character and reputation. Of the 5 percent that canceled, half of those cancellations were unrelated to BDS, such as those caused by scheduling problems or lack of ticket sales. Approximately 2.5 percent of scheduled performers did cancel as a direct result of BDS pressure, but only a small portion did so because their minds had been changed. Most of them, as previously noted, canceled out of fear for their careers or physical safety.

NEXT STEP: EXPRESS YOUR JOY AT ARTIST SUPPORT.

Do not engage in Twitter wars on the pages of artists who support Israel; be positive. Thank them for being ambassadors for peace.

Like their social media pages and follow them.

EPILOGUE

THE WAY FORWARD

The goal of the cultural boycott is the same as other forms of BDS—to delegitimize the Jewish state and promote Jew-hatred—but the effective way to counter the cultural boycott is radically different. Here we can go on the offense and bring the battle to BDS. When we reveal the cultural boycott strategies of intimidation, censorship, and blacklists and the antisemitic tropes underlying its false accusations against Israel, we focus on the morality of the cultural boycott itself. It is a winning argument that puts BDS on the defense.

For too long, the response from Israel's supporters has been almost exclusively defensive. While correcting the misinformation and lies inherent in the BDS narrative is important, it does not change the conversation or detract from the appeal that its propaganda has in numerous circles. In today's flood of media, debating "facts" only serves to create the false impression that the facts are unclear and our arguments are merely opinions of "the Zionists."

Going forward, we need to combine facts with emotion and personal perspective. Jews have a very specific world experience that includes thousands of years of persecution and mass genocide. We are disproportionately victims of hate crimes and hate speech. This has resulted in that sinking, awful feeling that we must always be careful and ready for the worst. Our trauma is intergenerational, our persecution real. Vicious attacks on the only Jewish homeland and chronic calls for its extinction heighten our insecurity.

Jews have always supported the civil rights of others, and like most other Jews, I am very proud of that. However, it is time to demand the same civil rights for ourselves and social consequences for those who stir up hatred against us.

Jews are being scapegoated on both the right and the left, and dangerous antisemitic speech receives a muted response or is brushed off and tolerated. This must change. We must demand equal treatment for Jews and social and legal consequences for the unique expression of hatred that threatens our safety. We warrant the same protections from provocative hate speech that social media platforms give to other minority groups. We must insist on balance from mainstream news publications.

I do not personally support "cancel culture," whereby people lose their jobs if they express a viewpoint that others think is offensive. I think that cancel culture represents a dangerous and easily abused tool. Many people have suffered ruined careers for decades-old comments and others for relatively innocuous comments.

However, we should hold artists and others accountable for

comments that are antisemitic and demand retractions and apologies. We do this simply by calling them out for their anti-Jewish hate speech. Public backlash works. Artists can and have recanted and apologized for hateful remarks. They delete posts, reducing the spread of disinformation. They can and do think more carefully about what they are saying after they face scrutiny. Some, like rapper and TV host Nick Cannon, even appear to truly atone and warrant our support. Acute backlash for one artist is a warning signal for others to think about what they are saying and endorsing. Traditional and social media circulate these stories as well and will help get the word out for us. Jew-hatred must once and for all become politically incorrect.

Recognizing Jew-hatred wherever it appears, and in whatever form, is the battle of all people everywhere who care about freedom, justice, and equality. We are living in a time of chaos and fear but also possibility. As other communities raise their voices across the country demanding positive change, so must we.

We are not alone; we have allies. This is not a Jewish fight. This is everyone's fight. Antisemitism is the canary in the coal mine and a poison pill for the whole world. When we stand up for ourselves, others will stand with us.

In his book *The Wicked Son*, author, screenwriter, director, and iconic playwright David Mamet observes that:[318]

> Many of us harbor fantasies about speaking up against the Nazi tyranny. How could the world not have spoken in 1933, in 1943, we ask? Were I alive then, we fantasize, I would have spoken...But we were not, or not of the age of reason, and we cannot "speak up" in the past. We can speak up *now*.

I am moved and guided by his words. A future without Jew-hatred begins with you and me.

HOW YOU CAN HELP:

If you found this book helpful and informative and its message important, recommend it to your friends.

Suggest this book to libraries and schools as high school and college reading.

If you like what I have to say, suggest I be invited to speak to your community, organization, company, school, or place of worship: www.LiberateArt.net or Bookings@LanaMelman.com.

Follow my social media, sign up for my newsletters, and when there is a call to action, join me in responding—numbers matter!

ENDNOTES

1   Matthew Kalman, "Oxfam under Pressure to Cut Ties with Scarlett Johansson over SodaStream Ad," *The Guardian*, January 29, 2014, https://www.theguardian.com/ society/2014/jan/29/oxfam-pressure-scarlett-johansson-sodastream-israel.

2   Roger Waters, "A Note from Roger–February 1, 2014," Facebook, February 1, 2014 (last modified May 5, 2021), https://m.facebook.com/nt/screen/?params=%7B%22note_ id%22%3A982827988898412%7D&path=%2Fnotes%2Fnote%2F&refsrc=deprecated&_rdr.

3   "Scarlett Johansson Fights Controversy, Justin Bieber's Chillin' in Panama," *ABC News*, January 28, 2014, https://abcnews.go.com/US/ social-climber-scarlett-johansson-fights-controversy/story?id=22261713.

4   Associated Press, "Scarlett Johansson Addresses Criticism over SodaStream Ad Campaign," *Hollywood Reporter*, January 25, 2014, https://www.hollywoodreporter.com/news/ general-news/scarlett-johansson-addresses-criticism-sodastream-674051.

5   Greg Gilman, "Scarlett Johansson Resigns Oxfam Role over 'Uncensored' Super Bowl Ad (Video)," *The Wrap*, January 30, 2014, https://www.thewrap.com/scarlett-johanssons- uncensored-super-bowl-sodastream-commercial-causes-rift-oxfam-charity.

6   David Brindle, "Oxfam Boss Admits Errors over Scarlett Johansson Row," *The Guardian*, December 15, 2016, https://www.theguardian.com/voluntary-sector-network/2016/dec/15/ oxfam-pr-disaster-scarlett-johansson-perfect-storm-tweet.

7   Ryan Rodrick Beiler, "SodaStream Admits Bowing to Boycott Pressure," *The Electronic Intifada*, February 22, 2016, https://electronicintifada.net/blogs/ryan-rodrick-beiler/ sodastream-admits-bowing-boycott-pressure.

8   JTA, "SodaStream Hires Hundreds of New Employees in Southern Israel," *The Times of Israel*, July 28, 2016, https://www.timesofisrael.com/sodastream-hires-hundreds-of-new-employees-in-southern-israel/; and Palestinian Boycott, Divestment, and Sanctions National Committee (BNC), "SodaStream Is Still Subject to Boycott," *BDS Movement*, August 22, 2018, https://bdsmovement.net/news/%E2%80%9Csodastream-still-subject-boycott%E2%80%9D.

9   Guinness World Records, "Best-Selling Female Recording Artist," GuinnessWorldRecords.com, March 23, 2015, https://www.guinnessworldrecords.com/world-records/best-selling-female-recording-artist.

10   "Cultural Impact of Madonna," *Wikipedia*, last modified December 30, 2021, https://en.wikipedia.org/wiki/Cultural_impact_of_Madonna.

11   Dana Hughes, "George Clooney Arrested at Sudanese Embassy," *ABC News*, March 16, 2012, https://abcnews.go.com/Politics/OTUS/george-clooney-arrested-sudan-embassy-washington-dc/story?id=15936415.

12   Maeve Shearlaw, "What Happened to Darfur after George Clooney Came to Town?" *The Guardian*, December 11, 2014, https://www.theguardian.com/world/2014/dec/11/-sp-george-cloony-darfur-what-next.

13   Jodi Cantor and Rachel Abrams, "Gwyneth Paltrow, Angelina Jolie, and Others Say Harvey Weinstein Harassed Them," *New York Times*, October 10, 2017, https://www.nytimes.com/2017/10/10/us/gwyneth-paltrow-angelina-jolie-harvey-weinstein.html.

14   Jodi Cantor and Rachel Abrams, "Gwyneth Paltrow, Angelina Jolie and Others Say Harvey Weinstein Harassed Them," *New York Times*, October 10, 2017, https://www.nytimes.com/2017/10/10/us/gwyneth-paltrow-angelina-jolie-harvey-weinstein.html.

15   Katie Reilly, "'No More.' Read Rose McGowan's First Public Remarks since Accusing Harvey Weinstein of Rape," *Time*, October 27, 2017, https://time.com/5000381/rose-mcgowan-harvey-weinstein-speech-transcript.

16   Ashley Judd (@@AshleyJudd), "Women who haven't had the opportunity to speak up yet, we have your back," Twitter, December 7, 2017, https://mobile.twitter.com/AshleyJudd/status/938831362492129281.

17   Uma Thurman (@@umathurman), "H A P P Y T H A N K S G I V I N G I am grateful today, to be alive, for all those I love, and for all those who have the courage to stand up for others. I said I was angry recently, and I have a few reasons, #metoo," Instagram, November 23, 2017, https://www.instagram.com/p/Bb2h0hBlV3T.

18   JTA, "Roger Waters Concert Features Nazi-Like Uniform, Pig Balloon with Jewish Symbol," *The Jerusalem Post*, July 25, 2013, https://www.jpost.com/International/Roger-Waters-concert-features-Nazi-like-uniform-pig-balloon-with-Jewish-symbol-321087.

19 Lana Melman, "Roger Waters (Pink Floyd) Comparing Jews to Aliens," YouTube, uploaded April 28, 2020, https://www.youtube.com/watch?v=hf_SK8MgF4o&list=PLVmtfcs5jtuRl5o4S8gHDj9hWI7bkGgWj&index=3.

20 Daniel Kreps, "Roger Waters Criticizes 'Whining' Thom Yorke over Radiohead's Israel Gig," *Rolling Stone*, July 16, 2017, https://www.rollingstone.com/music/music-news/roger-waters-criticizes-whining-thom-yorke-over-radioheads-israel-gig-197361.

21 Roger Waters, "Roger Waters to Dionne Warwick: 'You Are Showing Yourself to Be Profoundly Ignorant of What Has Happened in Palestine since 1947,'" *Salon*, May 14, 2015, https://www.salon.com/2015/05/14/roger_waters_to_dionne_warwick_you_are_showing_yourself_to_be_profoundly_ignorant_of_what_has_happened_in_palestine_since_1947.

22 Liat Collins, "We Don't Need No Education," *The Jerusalem Post*, June 20, 2019, https://www.jpost.com/bds-threat/we-dont-need-no-education-593108.

23 Simon Wiesenthal Center Reports, "2013 Top Ten Anti-Semitic/Anti-Israel Slurs," Simon Wiesenthal Center, 2013, http://bit.ly/2NKewwz.

24 Jonah Goldberg, "Structural Antisemitism," *The Dispatch*, May 19, 2021, https://gfile.thedispatch.com/p/structural-antisemitism.

25 Rose Ritch, "I Was Harassed and Persecuted on Campus Just for Being a Zionist," *Newsweek*, August 10, 2020, https://www.newsweek.com/i-was-harassed-persecuted-campus-just-being-zionist-opinion-1523873.

26 David Baddiel, *Jews Don't Count* (New York: HarperCollins Publishers, 2021), 92.

27 Andras Kovacs and Gyorgy Fischer, "European Antisemitism Survey: Antisemitic Prejudices in Europe," Action & Protection League, 2021, https://apleu.org/european-antisemitism-survey.

28 Emma Nolan, "Bella Hadid, Dua Lipa, and the Other Celebs Supporting Palestine over Israel," *Newsweek*, May 11, 2021, https://www.newsweek.com/palestine-celebrities-support-conflict-israel-bella-gigi-hadid-mark-ruffalo-dua-lipa-1590420.

29 Halsey (@@halsey), "It is not "too complicated to understand" that brown children are being murdered + people are being displaced under the occupation of one of the most powerful armies in the world," Twitter, May 12, 2021, https://twitter.com/halsey/status/1392534806584430595.

30 JNS, "Rosanna Arquette Alleges Israel Knew about Virus, Put 'Lives at Risk for Profit,'" *Jewish News Syndicate*, March 18, 2020, https://www.jns.org/rosanna-arquette-alleges-israel-knew-about-virus-put-lives-at-risk-for-profit.

31 Timothy Bella, "SNL's Michael Che Said Israel Only Vaccinated Its 'Jewish Half.' Critics Call the Joke 'An Antisemitic Trope,'" *The Washington Post*, Morning Mix, February 23, 2021, https://www.washingtonpost.com/nation/2021/02/23/michael-che-israel-vaccine-snl.

32   Maariv Online and Jerusalem Post Staff, "Dua Lipa Shares Anti-Israel Post on Instagram," *The Jerusalem Post*, June 2, 2020. https://www.jpost.com/israel-news/culture/pop-star-dua-lipa-shares-anti-israel-post-on-instagram-629955.

33   Mia Farrow (@@MiaFarrow), "Kids in Gaza," Twitter, May 11, 2021, https://twitter.com/MiaFarrow/status/1392135181188882434.

34   Benjamin W. Segel, *A Lie and a Libel: The History of the Protocols of the Elders of Zion*, trans. R. S. Levy (Lincoln: University of Nebraska Press, 1996), xi.

35   Benjamin W. Segel, *A Lie and a Libel: The History of the Protocols of the Elders of Zion*, trans. R. S. Levy (Lincoln: University of Nebraska Press, 1996), xii.

36   Joseph Levy, "ARABS BLAME RIOTS ON BROKEN PLEDGE; Grand Mufti Produces Letter by Balfour Backing Promises of Lawrence of Arabia. RIGHTS OF JEWS DENIED Moslem Leader Reiterates Claim to Ownership of Wailing Wall—'Protocols of Zion' in Evidence. Tells of British Pledge. Arab Stand Questioned. Balfour Letter Produced. 'Protocols of Zion' Cited," *New York Times*, December 4, 1929, https://www.nytimes.com/1929/12/04/archives/arabs-blame-riots-on-broken-pledge-grand-mufti-produces-letter-by.html.

37   "Today it is Palestine, tomorrow it will be one country or another. The Zionist plan is limitless. After Palestine, the Zionists aspire to expand from the Nile to the Euphrates. When they will have digested the region they overtook, they will aspire to further expansion, and so on. Their plan is embodied in the 'Protocols of the Elders of Zion', and their present conduct is the best proof of what we are saying."

"Hamas Covenant," Yale Law School Lillian Goldman Law Library, August 18, 1988, https://avalon.law.yale.edu/20th_century/hamas.asp.

38   Seth Cohen, "Nick Cannon's YouTube Show Causes Waves," *Forbes*, July 13, 2020, https://www.forbes.com/sites/sethcohen/2020/07/13/nick-cannon-spreads-anti-jewish-theories-criticizing-rothschilds-and-zionists/?sh=61d01d8410c8.

39   Francesca Bacardi, "ViacomCBS Has Rehired Nick Cannon to Host 'Wild 'N' Out,'" *PageSix.com*, February 5, 2021, https://pagesix.com/2021/02/05/nick-cannon-resumes-hosting-wild-n-out-after-apology.

40   Mairead McArdle, "Charlamagne Tha God Says Nick Cannon Was Fired Because Jews 'Have the Power,'" *National Review*, July 16, 2020, https://www.yahoo.com/now/charlamagne-tha-god-says-nick-184715407.html.

41   Lana Melman, "Nick Cannon Says 'It's Time to #EndJewHatred,'" *The Times of Israel*, December 2, 2020, https://blogs.timesofisrael.com/nick-cannon-says-its-time-to-endjewhatred.

42   Donna Rachel Edmunds, "Antisemitic Mural Resurfaces at March on Washington 2020," *The Jerusalem Post*, August 30, 2020, https://www.jpost.com/diaspora/antisemitism/antisemitic-mural-resurfaces-at-march-on-washington-2020-640435.

43 Kareem Abdul-Jabbar, "Kareem Abdul-Jabbar: Where Is the Outrage Over Anti-Semitism in Sports and Hollywood?" *HolleywoodReporter.com*, July 14, 2020, https://www.hollywoodreporter.com/lifestyle/lifestyle-news/kareem-abdul-jabbar-is-outrage-anti-semitism-sports-hollywood-1303210.

44 JTA and Gabe Freidman, "Doubling Down on Antisemitic Conspiracy Theories, Rapper Ice Cube Tweets Again—and Faces a Backlash," *Haaretz*, June 14, 2020, https://www.haaretz.com/us-news/doubling-down-on-antisemitic-conspiracy-theories-rapper-ice-cube-keeps-on-tweeting-1.8919932.

45 Josh Malina (@@JoshMalina), "Why's it so hard to get cancel culture on the line when the problem is antisemitism?" Twitter, July 7, 2020, https://twitter.com/JoshMalina/status/1280531251598725126?ref_src=twsrc%5Etfw%7Ctwcamp%5Etweetembed%7Ctwterm%5E1280531251598725126%7Ctwgr%5E%7Ctwcon%5Es1_&ref_url=https%3A%2F%2Fjewishjournal.com%2Fculture%2F318751%2Fjosh-malina-why-doesnt-cancel-culture-apply-to-anti-semitism%2F.

46 Kareem Abdul-Jabbar, "Kareem Abdul-Jabbar: Where Is the Outrage over Anti-Semitism in Sports and Hollywood?" *Hollywood Reporter*, July 14, 2020, https://www.hollywoodreporter.com/lifestyle/lifestyle-news/kareem-abdul-jabbar-is-outrage-anti-semitism-sports-hollywood-1303210.

47 Joseph Wulfsohn, "Ice Cube Fires Back at Kareem Abdul-Jabbar Column for Calling Out His Anti-Semitism," *Fox News*, July 15, 2020, https://www.foxnews.com/media/ice-cube-kareem-abdul-jabbar-column-anti-semitism.

48 FredWreck (@@Fredwreck), "Another backstabbing Emirati Ibn Gahba! The Shekhel is the new God #freepalestine," Twitter, October 18, 2020, https://twitter.com/Fredwreck/status/1317813304111239174.

49 Yashar Ali (@@yashar), "This is disgusting," Twitter, June 17, 2019, https://twitter.com/yashar/status/1140762303438176256.

50 Bari Weiss (@@bariweiss), "Gotta love Cusack's defense," Twitter, June 17, 2019, https://mobile.twitter.com/bariweiss/status/1140768580021018624?lang=fi.

51 Houston Keene, "Pakistani Actress Quotes Adolf Hitler to 1.2 Million Twitter Followers as Tensions Flare in Israel," *Fox News*, May 12, 2021, https://www.foxnews.com/entertainment/pakistani-actress-veena-malik-adolf-hitler-jews.

52 Ben Beaumont-Thomas, "Wiley Posts Antisemitic Tweets, Likening Jews to Ku Klux Klan," *The Guardian*, July 24, 2020, https://www.theguardian.com/music/2020/jul/24/wiley-accused-of-antisemitism-after-likening-jews-to-ku-klux-klan.

53 Elisha Fieldstadt, "ViacomCBS Cuts Ties with Nick Cannon after Anti-Semitic Comments," *NBC News*, July 15, 2020, https://www.nbcnews.com/pop-culture/celebrity/viacomcbs-cuts-ties-nick-cannon-after-anti-semitic-comments-n1233878.

54 "Almodóvar, Penélope Cruz o Bardem Denuncian el 'Genocidio' Israelí en la Franja de Gaza," *Europa Press*, July 28, 2014, https://www.europapress.es/cultura/cine-00128/noticia-almodovar-penelope-cruz-bardem-denuncian-genocidio-israeli-franja-gaza-20140728142255.html; and Ben Jones, "Penelope Cruz, Javier Bardem Denounce Israeli 'Genocide' in Open Letter," *Holleywood Reporter*, July 29, 2014, https://www.hollywoodreporter.com/movies/movie-news/penelope-cruz-javier-bardem-denounce-721894.

55 Dan Diker and Adam Shay, "The Money Trail: European Union Financing of Organizations Promoting Boycotts against the State of Israel," State of Israel Ministry of Strategic Affairs and Public Diplomacy, 2nd Edition, January 2019, https://www.gov.il/BlobFolder/generalpage/nativ010819/en/strategic_affairs_nativPDFeng010819.pdf.

56 The Lawfare Project provides pro bono legal services to protect the civil and human rights of the Jewish people worldwide: https://www.thelawfareproject.org.

57 In response, the US withdrew from the conference. Then-US Secretary of State Colin Powell's statement of withdrawal, in part: "Today I have instructed our representatives at the World Conference Against Racism to return home. I have taken this decision with regret, because of the importance of the international fight against racism and the contribution that the Conference could have made to it. But, following discussions today by our team in Durban and others who are working for a successful conference, I am convinced that will not be possible. I know that you do not combat racism by conferences that produce declarations containing hateful language, some of which is a throwback to the days of 'Zionism equals racism'; or supports the idea that we have made too much of the Holocaust; or suggests that apartheid exists in Israel; or that singles out only one country in the world—Israel—for censure and abuse." See "George W. Administration: US Withdraws from World Conference Against Racism," *Jewish Virtual Library*, accessed January 17, 2022, https://www.jewishvirtuallibrary.org/u-s-withdraws-from-world-conference-against-racism.

58 Elihai Braun, "UN World Conference against Racism, Radical Discrimination, Xenophobia and Related Intolerance—Durban, South Africa,'" *Jewish Virtual Library*, September, 2001, https://www.jewishvirtuallibrary.org/durban-i-un-conference-against-racism-2001.

59 BDS, "Palestinian BNC National Committee," accessed December 13, 2021, https://bdsmovement.net/bnc.

60 Israeli Apartheid Week, "Call Out: 15th Annual Israeli Apartheid Week," *BDSMovement.net*, February 28, 2019, https://bdsmovement.net/news/call-out-15th-annual-israeli-apartheid-week.

61 "Jewish Voice for Peace," *Wikipedia*, updated January 24, 2022, https://en.wikipedia.org/wiki/Jewish_Voice_for_Peace.

62 "Why We #BDS," Adalah-NY, accessed December 12, 2021, https://adalahny.org.

63 J. K. Rowling, Simon Schama, et al., "Israel Needs Cultural Bridges, Not Boycotts," *The Guardian*, October 22, 2015, https://www.theguardian.com/world/2015/oct/22/israel-needs-cultural-bridges-not-boycotts-letter-from-jk-rowling-simon-schama-and-others.

64 Daniel Kreps, "Rage Against the Machine, Serj Tankian, Roger Waters Sign Letter Asking Artists to Boycott Israel," *Rolling Stone*, May 27, 2021, https://www.rollingstone.com/music/music-news/rage-against-the-machine-serj-tankian-roger-waters-sign-open-letter-artists-boycott-israel-1175281.

65 "Our Names," Musicians for Palestine, accessed December 30, 2021, https://musiciansforpalestine.com/our-names.

66 Adalah-NY (@@AdalahNY), "We went to @@Brooklinen's new Williamsburg store to return their sheets. They were stained with Israeli apartheid," Twitter, February 23, 2020, https://twitter.com/AdalahNY/status/1231739445084381185.

67 Russell Brand, "Which Companies Invest in Gaza Violence?" YouTube, August 13, 2014, https://www.youtube.com/watch?v=E04vISi2nho.

68 "Israel-Palestine: This Is How It Ends," Avaaz, accessed December 14, 2021, https://secure.avaaz.org/campaign/en/israel_palestine_this_is_how_it_ends_loc.

69 "Thom Yorke Breaks Silence on Israel Controversy," *Rolling Stone*, June 2, 2017, https://www.rollingstone.com/music/music-news/thom-yorke-breaks-silence-on-israel-controversy-126675.

70 ISRAEL21c, accessed December 15, 2021, https://www.israel21c.org; The ISRAEL21c website is an excellent source for a lengthy list of Israel's academic and scientific contributions to the world.

71 "University and College Union," *Wikipedia*, updated December 11, 2021, https://en.wikipedia.org/wiki/University_and_College_Union.

72 Mitchell Bard, "The History of the Boycott, Divestment, Sanctions (BDS) Movement," *JewishVirtualLibrary.org*, accessed January 27, 2022, https://www.jewishvirtuallibrary.org/bds-movement#academic.

73 Associated Press, "Palestinian University President Comes Out Against Boycott of Israeli Academics," *Haaretz*, June 17, 2006, https://www.haaretz.com/1.4918044.

74 "Harvard President Condemns 'Anti-Semitic' Divestiture in Israel," *The Tufts Daily*, September 25, 2002, https://tuftsdaily.com/archives/2002/09/25/harvard-president-condemns-anti-semitic-divestiture-in-israel/; and Karen W. Arenson, "Harvard President Sees Rise in Anti-Semitism on Campus," *The New York Times*, September 21, 2002, https://www.nytimes.com/2002/09/21/us/harvard-president-sees-rise-in-anti-semitism-on-campus.html.

75 Benjamin Weinthal, "Academic Organization Votes to Reject BDS," *The Jerusalem Post*, August 22, 2019, https://www.jpost.com/BDS-THREAT/Society-for-the-Study-of-Social-Problems-rejects-BDS-599186.

76 Ben-Dror Yemini, *Industry of Lies: Media, Academia, and the Israeli-Arab Conflict* (United States: Institute for the Study of Global Antisemitism and Policy, 2017).

77 Ben-Dror Yemini, *Industry of Lies: Media, Academia, and the Israeli-Arab Conflict* (United States: Institute for the Study of Global Antisemitism and Policy, 2017), 69.

78 Rose Ritch, "I Was Harassed and Persecuted on Campus Just for Being a Zionist," *Newsweek*, August 10, 2020, https://www.newsweek.com/i-was-harassed-persecuted-campus-just-being-zionist-opinion-1523873.

79 Noah Browning, "Major Dutch Pension Firm Divests from Israeli Banks over Settlements," *Reuters*, January 8, 2014, https://www.reuters.com/article/netherlands-israel-divestment/major-dutch-pension-firm-divests-from-israeli-banks-over-settlements-idUSL6N0KI1N220140108.

80 JTA and TOI Staff, "Dutch Pensions Group Removes Israeli Banks from Blacklist," *The Times of Israel*, January 10, 2019, https://www.timesofisrael.com/dutch-pensions-group-removes-israeli-banks-from-blacklist.

81 "Anti-Semitism: Campus Divestment Resolutions in the USA (2005–2021)," Jewish Virtual Library, accessed December 14, 2021, https://www.jewishvirtuallibrary.org/campus-divestment-resolutions.

82 "Anti-Semitism: Campus Divestment Resolutions in the USA (2005–2021)," Jewish Virtual Library, accessed December 14, 2021, https://www.jewishvirtuallibrary.org/campus-divestment-resolutions.

83 "Anti-Semitism: Campus Divestment Resolutions in the USA (2005–2021)," Jewish Virtual Library, accessed December 14, 2021, https://www.jewishvirtuallibrary.org/campus-divestment-resolutions.

84 "UN Watch in the News–November 2021," *UNWatch.org*, December 22, 2021, https://unwatch.org/un-watch-in-the-news-november-2021.

85 "UNsurprising: The World Body Keeps Up Its Assault on Israel," *New York Daily News*, December 3, 2021, https://www.nydailynews.com/opinion/ny-edit-un-israel-20211203-2ynvm3ojb5cvnawpce4aq3el2q-story.html.

86 "The U.N. and Israel: Key Statistics from UN Watch," *UNWatch.org*, August 23, 2016, https://unwatch.org/un-israel-key-statistics.

87 Andrew Carey, "UN Publishes 'Blacklist' of Companies Doing Business in Israeli Settlements," *CNN*, updated February 12, 2020, https://www.cnn.com/2020/02/12/middleeast/un-blacklist-israel-settlements-intl/index.html.

88 Afghanistan, Albania, Algeria, Azerbaijan, Bahrain, Bangladesh, Benin, Brunei Darussalam, Burkina Faso, Cameroon, Chad, Comoros, Côte D'Ivoire, Djibouti, Egypt, Gabon, Gambia, Guinea, Guinea-Bissau, Guyana, Indonesia, Iran, Iraq, Jordan, Kazakhstan, Kuwait, Kyrgyz Republic, Lebanon, Libyan Arab Jamahiriya, Malaysia, Maldives, Mali, Mauritania, Morocco, Mozambique, Niger, Nigeria, Oman, Pakistan, Qatar, Saudi Arabia, Senegal, Sierra Leone, Somalia, Sudan, Suriname, Syrian Arab Republic, Tajikistan, Togo, Tunisia, Turkey, Turkmenistan, Uganda, United Arab Emirates, Uzbekistan, Yemen.

89 Lahav Harkov, "BDS Founder: If Israel Develops Coronavirus Vaccine You Can Take It," *The Jerusalem Post*, April 6, 2020, https://www.jpost.com/Israel-News/ BDS-founder-No-need-to-boycott-Israeli-developed-coronavirus-drugs-623759.

90 "List of Universities and Colleges in the State of Palestine," *Wikipedia*, last modified September 2, 2021, https://en.wikipedia.org/wiki/ List_of_universities_and_colleges_in_the_State_of_Palestine.

91 Nikki Golomb, "Omar Barghouti: A Man with Two Faces," Jerusalem Institute of Justice, February 6, 2018, https://jij.org/news/omar-barghouti-man-two-faces.

It appears that Baghouti has been working on his PhD for years, which is not unusual. I was not able to find any sources that indicate the doctorate had been completed.

92 Dag Hammarskjöld Society, "Omar Barghouti—Strategies for Change," Vimeo, September 23, 2013, https://vimeo.com/75201955. See time stamp 5:53 for relevant content.

93 Dag Hammarskjöld Society, "Omar Barghouti—Strategies for Change," Vimeo, September 23, 2013, https://vimeo.com/75201955. See time stamp 5:23 for relevant content.

94 Dag Hammarskjöld Society, "Omar Barghouti—Strategies for Change," Vimeo, September 23, 2013, https://vimeo.com/75201955. See time stamp 5:23 for relevant content.

95 "The Boycott, Divestment and Sanctions (BDS) Movement Unmasked," Creative Community for Peace, accessed March 4, 2022, https://www.creativecommunityforpeace. com/about-bds/.

96 Stand with Us, "What is the boycott movement against Israel? It's a movement driven by fanatic hatred," Facebook video, https://fb.watch/9IG19VQEPR.

97 Charlie Crooijmans, "Salif Keita Pressured to Cancel Jerusalem Sacred Music Festival," News and Noise, August 23, 2013, https://newsandnoise.nl/2013/08/ salif-keita-pressured-to-cancel-jerusalem-sacred-music-festival.

98 "Islamic Leader Threatens McCartney over TA Show," *The Jerusalem Post*, September 14, 2008, https://www.jpost.com/international/ islamic-leader-threatens-mccartney-over-ta-show.

99 "Threats Force Eric Burdon to Cancel Israel Show," Vintage Vinyl News, July 25, 2013, https:// www.vintagevinylnews.com/2013/07/threats-force-eric-burdon-to-cancel.html.

100 Benjamin of Tudela (@@BenjaminTudela), "@@Israellycool on page 35 of todays Yisrael Hayom Burdon states (my trans): 'it wasn't my decision to cancel the show, but that of my manager, following numerous threatening emails, she was scared for my life,'" Twitter, July 31, 2013, https://twitter.com/BenjaminTudela/status/362543559842344961.

101 Michael James, "Demonizing the Enemy a Hallmark of War," ABC News, January 6, 2006, https://abcnews.go.com/International/story?id=79071.

102 "Spanish Festival Flipflops on Ban, Re-Invites Matisyahu," The Times of Israel, August 19, 2015, https://www.timesofisrael.com/spanish-festival-flipflops-on-ban-re-invites-matisyahu.

103 Alex Ritman, "Eddie Izzard Misses Palestinian Marathon Following Backlash over Tel Aviv Gig," Hollywood Reporter, March 31, 2017, https://www.hollywoodreporter.com/news/eddie-izzard-misses-palestinian-marathon-backlash-tel-aviv-gig-990326.

104 "Eddie Izzard Pulls Out of Palestine Marathon," Chortle, March 31, 2017, https://www.chortle.co.uk/news/2017/03/31/27204/eddie_izzard_pulls_out_of_palestine_marathon.

105 "The Martha Wainwright Visit," Hebden Bridge Web, November 25, 2014, http://www.hebdenbridge.co.uk/news/2014/244.html.

106 "Hebden Bridge Martha Wainwright Show Embroiled in Israeli Boycott Row," Halifax Courier, November 21, 2014, https://www.halifaxcourier.co.uk/lifestyle/hebden-bridge-martha-wainwright-show-embroiled-israeli-boycott-row-2612381?amp.

107 "Martha Wainwright, Everything Wrong with Israeli Apartheid," Facebook, https://www.facebook.com/Martha.Wainwright.Apartheid.Israel.Wrong.

108 Jane Coaston, "The Intersectionality Wars," Vox, May 28, 2019, https://www.vox.com/the-highlight/2019/5/20/18542843/intersectionality-conservatism-law-race-gender-discrimination.

109 Merrill Perlman, "The Origin of the Term 'Intersectionality,'" Columbia Journalism Review, October 23, 2018, https://www.cjr.org/language_corner/intersectionality.php.

110 David Baddiel, Jews Don't Count, (New York: HarperCollins Publishers, 2021), p 17.

111 David Baddiel, Jews Don't Count, (New York: HarperCollins Publishers, 2021), p 18.

112 Jeremy Ben-Ami, Lara Friedman, and Todd Gitlin, "BDS: An In-Depth Conversation," Partners for Progressive Israel, March 26, 2019, https://www.progressiveisrael.org/bds-an-in-depth-conversation/.

113 "Ancient Jewish History: The Philistines," Jewish Virtual Library, accessed December 15, 2021, https://www.jewishvirtuallibrary.org/the-philistines.

114 Herzl is credited as the founder of the Zionist movement by most historians, although several groups, including Hovevei Zion, were forerunners. https://mfa.gov.il/MFA/ AboutIsrael/History/Zionism/Pages/ZIONISM-%20Timeline%20of%20Events.aspx.

115 "Jewish Land Purchase in Palestine," *Wikipedia*, last modified December 14, 2021, https:// en.wikipedia.org/wiki/Jewish_land_purchase_in_Palestine.

116 Noa Tishby, *Israel—A Simple Guide to the Most Misunderstood Country on Earth* (New York, Free Press: 2021), 45.

117 Noa Tishby, *Israel—A Simple Guide to the Most Misunderstood Country on Earth* (New York, Free Press: 2021), 105.

118 "Palestine and the Palestinians (1948–67)," *Encyclopaedia Britannica*, accessed December 14, 2021, https://www.britannica.com/place/Palestine/Palestine-and-the-Palestinians-1948-67.

119 "Peel Commission: British History," *Encyclopaedia Britannica*, last modified September 3, 2010, https://www.britannica.com/event/Peel-Commission#ref988975.

120 "Peel Commission: British History," *Encyclopaedia Britannica*, last modified September 3, 2010, https://www.britannica.com/event/Peel-Commission#ref988975.

121 "Peel Commission: British History," *Encyclopaedia Britannica*, last modified September 3, 2010, https://www.britannica.com/event/Peel-Commission#ref988975.

122 "Green Line (Israel)," *Wikipedia*, last modified January 3, 2022,https://en.wikipedia.org/wiki/ Green_Line_(Israel).

123 "History of Jerusalem: Jordanian Annexation of the West Bank (April 24, 1950)," Jewish Virtual Library, accessed December 14, 2021, https://www.jewishvirtuallibrary.org/ jordanian-annexation-of-the-west-bank-april-1950.

124 Jay Sekulow, "UNRWA Has Changed the Definition of Refugee," *Foreign Policy*, August 17, 2018, https://foreignpolicy.com/2018/08/17/unrwa-has-changed-the-definition-of-refugee.

125 https://www.unrwa.org/who-we-are. The Palestinians are also the only people in the world who have a dedicated UN refugee agency—UNRWA. Every other refugee in the world is helped by the UN High Commission for Refugees (UNHCR).

126 "Khartoum Resolution," *Wikipedia*, accessed December 13, 2021, https://en.wikipedia.org/ wiki/Khartoum_Resolution.

127 Mitchell G. Bard, "Facts about Jewish Settlements in the West Bank," Jewish Virtual Library, accessed December 14, 2021, https://www.jewishvirtuallibrary.org/ facts-about-jewish-settlements-in-the-west-bank.

128 "The Palestinian Authority: History and Overview," Jewish Virtual Library, accessed January 17, 2022, https://www.jewishvirtuallibrary.org/palestinian-authority-history-and-overview.

129 "Fact Sheets: A 'Provisional' Palestinian State," Jewish Virtual Library, updated June 2002, https://www.jewishvirtuallibrary.org/a-ldquo-provisional-rdquo-palestinian-state.

130 Alan Dershowitz, *The Case for Israel* (New Jersey: Wiley Publishing, 2003), 8–9.

131 Nidal al-Mughrabi, "Gaza Fighting Descends into New Brutality," *Reuters*, June 12, 2007, https://www.reuters.com/article/us-palestinians-gaza-scene/gaza-fighting-descends-into-new-brutality-idUSL1264188820070612.

132 I have seen numerous letters he has sent; Lana Melman, "Cyndi Lauper Just Wants to Bring People Together," *The Times of Israel*, March 2, 2014, https://blogs.timesofisrael.com/cyndi-lauper-just-wants-to-bring-people-together.

133 David Lange, "Roger Waters Try to Project His Israel Hatred on to Alan Parsons. Fails Miserably (Updated)," *IsraellyCool*, February 8, 2015, https://www.israellycool.com/2015/02/08/roger-waters-try-to-project-his-israel-hatred-on-to-alan-parsons-fails-miserably.

134 "Alan Parsons Celebrates Bar Mitzva of Bass Player's Son in Jerusalem," *The Jerusalem Post*, November 10, 2017, https://www.jpost.com/israel-news/alan-parsons-celebrates-bar-mitzva-of-bass-players-son-in-jerusalem-513801.

135 Viva Sarah Press, "Jon Bon Jovi 'Excited' by Upcoming Tel Aviv Concert," ISRAEL21c, September 17, 2015, https://www.israel21c.org/jon-bon-jovi-excited-for-upcoming-tel-aviv-concert.

136 Viva Sarah Press, "Jon Bon Jovi 'Excited' by Upcoming Tel Aviv Concert," ISRAEL21c, September 17, 2015, https://www.israel21c.org/jon-bon-jovi-excited-for-upcoming-tel-aviv-concert.

137 Roger Waters, "Roger Waters to Jon Bon Jovi: 'You Stand Shoulder to Shoulder with the Settler Who Burned the Baby,'" *Salon*, October 2, 2015, https://www.salon.com/2015/10/02/roger_waters_to_jon_bon_jovi_you_stand_shoulder_to_shoulder_with_the_settler_who_burned_the_baby.

138 Frederik Pleitgen, "Israeli Court: American Protester Rachel Corrie's Death an Accident," *CNN*, September 4, 2012, https://www.cnn.com/2012/08/28/world/meast/israel-rachel-corrie-verdict/index.html.

139 *Walled Horizons* (Jerusalem: United Nations Office for the Coordination of Humanitarian Affairs [OCHA], 2009), documentary.

140 Gideon Levy, "Roger Waters Sets the Record Straight: I Hate Apartheid, Not Israel," *Haaretz*, August 2, 2015, updated April 10, 2018, https://www.haaretz.com/roger-waters-sets-the-record-straight-1.5381170.

141 Frank Barak, "An Interview with Roger Waters," *CounterPunch*, December 6, 2013, https://www.counterpunch.org/2013/12/06/an-interview-with-pink-floyds-roger-waters.

142 Kory Grow, "Howard Stern Blasts Roger Waters over Israel Boycott," *Rolling Stone*, October 6, 2015, https://www.rollingstone.com/music/music-news/howard-stern-blasts-roger-waters-over-israel-boycott-54823.

143 Gideon Levy, "Roger Waters Sets the Record Straight: I Hate Apartheid, Not Israel," *Haaretz*, August 2, 2015, updated April 10, 2018, https://www.haaretz.com/roger-waters-sets-the-record-straight-1.5381170.

144 David Hirsh, "Breaking Down the Wall," *The Guardian*, June 22, 2006, https://www.theguardian.com/commentisfree/2006/jun/22/rogerwatersdefiestheboycot.

145 "The Security Barrier," Anti-Defamation League, accessed December 14, 2021, https://www.adl.org/resources/glossary-terms/the-security-barrier.

146 Merav Yudilovitch, "Roger Waters Slams Israeli Occupation," *YNET News*, March 6, 2009, https://www.ynetnews.com/articles/0,7340,L-3725439,00.html.

147 Al Jazeera English, "Riz Khan—Walls of Separation," YouTube, March 4, 2011, https://www.youtube.com/watch?v=UdX5WpRrwtM.

148 Roger Waters, "Tear Down This Israeli Wall," *The Guardian*, March 11, 2011, https://www.theguardian.com/commentisfree/2011/mar/11/cultural-boycott-west-bank-wall.

149 Jon Blistein, "Roger Waters Calls for Boycott of Israel," *Rolling Stone*, March 20, 2013, https://www.rollingstone.com/music/music-news/roger-waters-calls-for-boycott-of-israel-65804.

150 Wilshire Boulevard Temple, "Defending Artistic Expression," YouTube, October 31, 2017, https://www.youtube.com/watch?v=S6KU9wRSYR8.

151 Aaron Bandler, "Disturbed Lead Singer Criticizes Roger Waters, BDS," *Jewish Journal*, June 4, 2019, https://jewishjournal.com/news/united-states/299535/disturbed-lead-singer-criticizes-roger-waters-bds.

152 Larry Derfner, "Roger Waters Discusses Boycott with Israel's 'Newspaper of the Nation,'" +972 *Magazine*, September 20, 2013, https://www.972mag.com/roger-waters-meets-israels-newspaper-of-the-nation.

153 David Seidenberg, "Roger Waters Claims Israeli Fans Nixed Peace. It's A Lie," *The Times of Israel*, June 11, 2019, https://blogs.timesofisrael.com/roger-waters-claims-israeli-fans-nixed-peace-its-a-lie/?fbclid=IwAR2kNrtnBERL1mqYgN7y5I4So6JAb7HInTerOgcGkdBOKl6iWQzuhxE-FVU.

154 The Mudman, "Roger Waters (Pink Floyd) ITN News Feature in Israel (2006)," YouTube, May 28, 2014, https://www.youtube.com/watch?v=-ArsL-dlgsk.

155 Gideon Levy, "Roger Waters Sets the Record Straight: I Hate Apartheid, Not Israel," *Haaretz*, August 2, 2015, updated April 10, 2018, https://www.haaretz.com/roger-waters-sets-the-record-straight-1.5381170.

156 Paul Gallagher, "Roger Waters: Pink Floyd Star on Why His Fellow Musicians Are Terrified to Speak Out against Israel," *The Independent,* February 19, 2016, https://www.independent. co.uk/news/people/roger-waters-pink-floyd-israel-boycott-ban-palestine-a6884971.html.

157 Reuters, "Roger Waters Broadcasts Cancelled in Germany over Support for Israel Boycott," *The Guardian,* November 28, 2017, https://www.theguardian.com/music/2017/nov/29/ roger-waters-broadcasts-cancelled-in-germany-over-accusations-of-antisemitism.

158 Samantha J. Gross, "Miami Beach Teens Will No Longer Perform with Roger Waters Due to Anti-Israel Controversy," *Miami Herald,* July 14, 2017, https://www.miamiherald.com/news/ local/community/miami-dade/miami-beach/article161195163.html.

159 Associated Press, "Jewish Advocacy Org Criticizes MLB Promotion of Roger Waters," Your Basin, January 30, 2020, https://www.yourbasin.com/sports/ jewish-advocacy-org-criticizes-mlb-promotion-of-roger-waters.

160 Lana Melman, "Roger Waters's Response to His Critics," YouTube, June 9, 2020, https://www. youtube.com/watch?v=nVYPYbH9nCY.

161 "Sour Note: Rolling Stones Perform in Israel, to the Chagrin of Pink Floyd," CBS News, June 5, 2014, https://www.cbsnews.com/news/ rolling-stones-perform-in-israel-despite-pink-floyds-boycott.

162 Brian Eno, "Brian Eno Compares Gaza Situation to Holocaust," Synthtopia, January 6, 2009, https://www.synthtopia.com/content/2009/01/06/ brian-eno-compares-gaza-situation-to-holocaust.

163 Dimple Vijaykumar, "Brian Eno Condemns Israeli Action in Gaza as 'Ethnic Cleansing,'" *The Guardian,* July 31, 2014, https://www.theguardian.com/music/2014/jul/31/ brian-eno-israel-palestine-gaza-ethnic-cleansing.

164 Peter Schwartz, "Gaza and the Loss of Civilization," *DavidByrne.com,* July 28, 2014, http:// davidbyrne.com/journal/gaza-and-the-loss-of-civilization.

165 Frank Barat, "Roger Waters and Brian Eno in Conversation: Music and Politics under COVID-19 Lockdown," Soundcloud, May 28, 2020, in *Covid-19 Chronicles* podcast, https://soundcloud.com/frank-barat/ roger-waters-brian-eno-in-conversation-music-and-politics-under-covid-19-lockdown.

166 "Singer Thurston Moore Says Support for BDS Led to Cancellation of Israel Gig," *Ynet,* June 27, 2015, https://www.ynetnews.com/articles/0,7340,L-4673222,00.html.

167 James Rettig, "Thurston Moore Issues Statement Supporting Israel Boycott," *Stereogum,* June 26, 2015, https://www.stereogum.com/1811823/ thurston-moore-issues-statement-supporting-israel-boycott/news.

168 Palestinian Campaign for the Academic and Cultural Boycott of Israel, "Palestinians, Thurston Moore Call on Dinosaur Jr. to Cancel Apartheid Israel Concert," BDSMovement. net, March 17, 2020, https://bdsmovement.net/news/dinosaur-jr.

169 Ghada Karmi, "Our Patrons," Palestine Solidarity Campaign, accessed March 12, 2022, https://www.palestinecampaign.org/about/patrons/.

170 Christopher Hart, "'The Stone and Seven Jewish Children: A Play for Gaza at the Royal Court, SW1," The Times, February 15, 2009, https://www.thetimes.co.uk/article/ the-stone-and-seven-jewish-children-a-play-for-gaza-at-the-royal-court-sw1-kx78rwrqzg8.

171 Michael Rosser, "Ken Loach Calls for Israel Boycott," ScreenDaily, August 22, 2014, https://www.screendaily.com/news/ken-loach-calls-for-israel-boycott/5076553. article?blocktitle=LATEST-FILM-NEWS&contentID=40562.

172 Mark Savage, "Radiohead on Israel Gig: 'Playing a Country Isn't the Same as Endorsing Its Government," BBC, July 12, 2017, https://www.bbc.com/news/entertainment-arts-40580326.

173 "BDS Activist and Radiohead Critic Ken Loach Slammed for Screening His Films across Israel," Haaretz, last modified April 24, 2018, https://www.haaretz.com/israel-news/ bds-activist-ken-loach-slammed-for-screening-his-films-across-israel-1.5431139.

174 "Ken Loach Calls for an Israel Boycott, But Perhaps Not for His Films," The Times of Israel, July 15, 2017, https://www.timesofisrael.com/ ken-loach-calls-for-an-israel-boycott-but-not-for-his-films.

175 Lee Harpin, "Loach: Labour MPs Who Protested against Antisemitism Should Be 'Kicked Out," The Jewish Chronicle, April 11, 2018, https://www.thejc.com/news/uk/kick-them-out- ken-loach-demands-removal-of-labour-mps-who-attended-antisemitism-rally-1.462090.

176 Lamiat Sabin, "Loach Slams Panorama Documentary as a 'Dishonest Hack Job,'" Morning Star, July 19, 2019, https://morningstaronline.co.uk/article/b/ loach-slams-panorama-documentary-as-a-dishonest-hatchet-job.

177 Alex Ritman, "Ken Loach's Expulsion from U.K.'s Labour Party Sparks Anger," Hollywood Reporter, August 16, 2021, https://www.hollywoodreporter.com/movies/movie-news/ ken-loachs-expulsion-from-u-k-s-labour-party-sparks-anger-1234998091.

178 "David Icke," Wikipedia, last updated December 23, 2021, https://en.wikipedia.org/wiki/ David_Icke.

179 Talya Zax, "Alice Walker Endorsed a Book by an AntiSemite in the New York Times," Haaretz, December 18, 2018, https://www.haaretz.com/us-news/ alice-walker-endorsed-a-book-by-an-anti-semite-in-the-new-york-times-1.6759882.

180 Agence France-Presse, "Lauryn Hill Cancels Israel Show after Cultural Boycott Pressure," The Guardian, May 4, 2015, https://www.theguardian.com/music/2015/may/05/ lauryn-hill-cancels-israel-show-after-cultural-boycott-pressure.

181 Ms. Lauryn Hill (@@mslaurynhill), "Dear Friends and Fans in Israel," Facebook, May 4, 2015, https://www.facebook.com/mslaurynhill/posts/1055564387804576.

182 Street Art United States, "When I See Them, I See Us," YouTube, filmed March 7, 2021, accessed December 15, 2021, https://www.youtube.com/watch?v=F5RY4MjdoXM.

183 JTA, "Lauryn Hill Appears in Activist Video Equating Treatment of US Blacks and Palestinians," *The Jerusalem Post*, October 18, 2015, https://www.jpost.com/israel-news/culture/lauryn-hill-appears-in-activist-video-comparing-us-racism-and-treatment-of-palestinians-426274.

184 JTA, "Ethiopian-Israeli Wins Miss Israel Pageant for First Time," *The Forward*, February 27, 2013, https://forward.com/news/breaking-news/172027/ethiopian-israeli-wins-miss-israel-pageant-for-fir.

185 Agencies, "Banksy's Nativity—with Bullet Hole in Place of Star—Unveiled in Bethlehem," *The Guardian*, December 22, 2019, https://www.theguardian.com/artanddesign/2019/dec/22/banksy-nativity-with-bullet-hole-in-place-of-star-unveiled-in-bethlehem.

186 Bethlehem is in the Palestinian-controlled West Bank; Sabrina Toppa, "Watch a Video of British Artist Banksy in Gaza," *Time*, February 26, 2015, https://time.com/3723390/banksy-video-gaza.

187 Damian P. *TripAdvisor.com*, posted January 2020, accessed December 15, 2021, https://www.tripadvisor.com/Hotel_Review-g293978-d12220602-Reviews-or10-The_Walled_Off_Hotel-Bethlehem_West_Bank.html#REVIEWS. The phrase "the worst view in the world" does not come from the poster originally; The Walled Off Hotel itself touts this as a tongue-in-cheek selling point.

188 The Palestinians claimed that the child—who became an overnight martyr—was shot by an Israeli sniper and died from bullet wounds. This much-publicized incident was caught on film by a freelance Palestinian journalist and broadcast on France 2 television. See "RAW FOOTAGE—Muhamad Al-Durrah Incident," YouTube video, 3:12, May 22, 2013, https://www.youtube.com/watch?v=arRgkXDLwlM.

Philippe Karsenty, a French media commentator, challenged the account and proposed that the bullets could not have come from the Israeli side given the IDF's position on the ground. See Cnaan Liphshiz, "Years after Infamous Intifada 'Hoax,' French-Jewish Crusader Fights On," *Times of Israel*, November 14, 2012, https://www.timesofisrael.com/years-after-infamous-intifada-hoax-french-jewish-crusader-fights-on/. More importantly, he questioned whether the child was killed. The video does not appear to show visible wounds on the child or blood at the scene, which is highly unlikely if someone dies of gunshot wounds. In addition, Karsenty alleged that France 2 had cut a few seconds off the end in which Muhammad appeared to lift his hand from his face after he had "died." See JTA, "Karsenty Convicted of Defamation in al-Dura Case," *The Jerusalem Post*, June 26, 2013, https://www.jpost.com/international/french-court-convicts-karsenty-of-defamation-in-al-dura-case-317849.

Israel initially took responsibility for the shooting of al-Dura, but a subsequent Israeli government investigation also questioned the death saying, "Contrary to [France 2's] claim that the boy is killed, the committee's review of the raw footage showed that in the final scenes, which were not broadcast by France 2, the boy is seen to be alive." "Frenchman Guilt of Defamation in Mohammed al-Dura Case," BBC News, June 27, 2013, https://www.bbc.com/news/world-middle-east-23075865.

The veracity of the alleged killing by Israeli snipers continues to be contested and a source of anti-Israeli sentiment. See "Shooting of 12-Year-Old Muhammad al-Dura 'staged', claims Israeli Report," YouTube video, 2:14, May 21, 2013, https://www.youtube.com/watch?v=xgsm9okPHG8; "Muhammad al-Durrah: The Image That Shocked the World," YouTube video, 1:34, September 30, 2020, https://www.youtube.com/watch?v=4NNz_FHCaBg.

A Defamation case against Mr. Karsenty by France 2 for accusing it of broadcasting a stages scene as news was at first upheld, then reversed, before he was ultimately convicted of defamation and ordered to pay a fine. "Media Analyst Convicted Over France-2 Palestinian Boy Footage," *The Guardian*, June 26, 2013, https://www.theguardian.com/world/2013/jun/26/france-2-palestinian-boy-footage)

Al-Dura's name has been spelled differently by various media outlets.

189 Ellie Duke, "Navajo Artist Creates Controversial Pro-Palestinian Mural on Santa Fe's Eastside," Hyperallergic, January 14, 2020, https://hyperallergic.com/537170/navajo-artist-creates-controversial-pro-palestinian-mural-on-santa-fes-eastside.

190 Ellie Duke, "Navajo Artist Creates Controversial Pro-Palestinian Mural on Santa Fe's Eastside," Hyperallergic, January 14, 2020, https://hyperallergic.com/537170/navajo-artist-creates-controversial-pro-palestinian-mural-on-santa-fes-eastside.

191 Mark Ruffalo (@@MarkRuffalo), "I have reflected & wanted to apologize for posts during the recent Israel/Hamas fighting," Twitter, May 24, 2021, https://twitter.com/markruffalo/status/1397023731722113032?lang=en.

192 Tamar Sternthal, "AFP Falsely Reports Lenny Kravitz Boycotted Israel," Committee for Accuracy in Middle East Reporting and Analysis, June 12, 2013, https://www.camera.org/article/afp-falsely-reports-lenny-kravitz-boycotted-israel.

193 Professor Kontorovich was discussing the status of the Golan Heights, but the principle applies to all the territory gained by Israel in the Six-Day War; Eugene Kontorovich, "International Law and the Recognition of Israeli Sovereignty in the Golan Heights," hearing before the US House of Representatives Committee on Oversight Subcommittee on National Security, July 17, 2018, https://docs.house.gov/meetings/GO/GO06/20180717/108563/HHRG-115-GO06-Wstate-KontorovichE-20180717.pdf.

194 "The IDF Code of Ethics," Approaching Conflicts, accessed December 15, 2021, https://toolkit.theicenter.org/content/idf-code-ethics.

195 Liel Leibovitz, "Some Concrete Facts about Hamas," *Tablet*, July 22, 2014, https://www.tabletmag.com/sections/israel-middle-east/articles/concrete-facts-about-hamas.

196 Ben-Dror Yemini, *Industry of Lies: Media, Academia, and the Israeli-Arab Conflict* (United States: Institute for the Study of Global Antisemitism and Policy, 2017), Chapter 15.

197 Ben-Dror Yemini, *Industry of Lies: Media, Academia, and the Israeli-Arab Conflict* (United States: Institute for the Study of Global Antisemitism and Policy, 2017), Chapter 15.

198 Khaleda Rahman, "John Oliver Accuses Israel of 'War Crimes,' Says US Should Reconsider Its Stance," *Newsweek*, May 17, 2021, https://www.newsweek.com/john-oliver-accuses-israel-war-crimes-us-reconsider-stance-1591977.

199 Khaleda Rahman, "John Oliver Accuses Israel of 'War Crimes,' Says US Should Reconsider Its Stance," *Newsweek*, May 17, 2021, https://www.newsweek.com/john-oliver-accuses-israel-war-crimes-us-reconsider-stance-1591977.

200 David Horovitz, "Jon Stewart—So Funny, So Wrong on Israel-Gaza," *The Times of Israel*, July 16, 2014, https://www.timesofisrael.com/jon-stewart-so-funny-so-wrong-on-israel-gaza.

201 David Horovitz, "Jon Stewart—So Funny, So Wrong on Israel-Gaza," *The Times of Israel*, July 16, 2014, https://www.timesofisrael.com/jon-stewart-so-funny-so-wrong-on-israel-gaza.

202 "Attacking Hezbollah's Financial Network: Policy Options," Hearing Before the Committee on Foreign Affairs House of Representatives, June 8, 2017, https://www.govinfo.gov/content/pkg/CHRG-115hhrg25730/html/CHRG-115hhrg25730.htm#:~:text=Hezbollah%20has%20long%20received%20hundreds%20of%20millions%20of%20dollars%20%0Aa%20year%20from%20Iran

203 Emma Nolan, "Bella Hadid, Dua Lipa, and the Other Celebs Supporting Palestine over Israel," *Newsweek*, May 11, 2021, https://www.newsweek.com/palestine-celebrities-support-conflict-israel-bella-gigi-hadid-mark-ruffalo-dua-lipa-1590420.

204 Sergio DellaPergola, "World Jewish Population, 2019," *American Jewish Year Book 2019* 119 (2020), https://doi.org/10.1007/978-3-030-40371-3_8.

205 "Myths & Facts Online—Human Rights in Israel and the Territories," Jewish Virtual Library, accessed December 15, 2021, https://www.jewishvirtuallibrary.org/myths-and-facts-online-human-rights-in-israel-and-the-territories#0.

206 "Palestinian Population 2021 (Live)," World Population Review, accessed December 30, 2021, https://worldpopulationreview.com/countries/palestine-population.

207 "Israel's Humanitarian Aid in Gaza," *JewishVirtualLibrary.org*, accessed January 27, 2022, https://www.jewishvirtuallibrary.org/israel-8217-s-humanitarian-aid-in-gaza.

208 "Please Tell Celine Dion: Don't Perform in Israel," CJPME, accessed December 15, 2021, https://www.cjpme.org/dont_go_celine.

209 "An Open Letter to Radiohead," APUK, April 23, 2017, https://artistsforpalestine.org. uk/2017/04/23/an-open-letter-to-radiohead.

210 "An Open Letter to Radiohead," APUK, April 23, 2017, https://artistsforpalestine.org. uk/2017/04/23/an-open-letter-to-radiohead.

211 Andy Greene, "Thom Yorke Breaks Silence on Israel Controversy," *Rolling Stone*, June 2, 2017, https://www.rollingstone.com/music/music-news/ thom-yorke-breaks-silence-on-israel-controversy-126675.

212 Nadia Abu-Shanab and Justine Sachs, "Dear Lorde, Here's Why We're Urging You Not to Play Israel," *The Spinoff*, December 21, 2017, https://thespinoff.co.nz/society/21-12-2017/ dear-lorde-heres-why-were-urging-you-not-to-play-israel.

213 Amy Spiro, "Is Lorde Canceling Israel Concert?" *The Jerusalem Post*, December 24, 2017, https://www.jpost.com/bds-threat/is-lorde-canceling-israel-concert-519783.

214 Eran Arielli, "Lorde's concert did not go off the site," Facebook, December 24, 2017, https:// www.facebook.com/eran.arielli/posts/10155472012697224?pnref=story.

215 Alice Walker, "Open Letter from Alice Walker to Alicia Keys: Don't Perform in Israel," *The New York Amsterdam News*, May 31, 2013, https://amsterdamnews.com/news/2013/05/31/ open-letter-from-alice-walker-to-alicia-keys-dont.

216 Times of Israel Staff, "Alicia Keys to Perform in Israel Despite Boycott Calls," *The Times of Israel*, June 1, 2013, https://www.timesofisrael.com/ alicia-keys-to-perform-in-israel-despite-boycott-calls.

217 Iyana Robertson, "Power Couplin': Beyonce, Jay-Z, Swizz Beatz, & Alicia Keys Hit The 2014 Global Citizen Festival," *Vibe.com*, September 28, 2014, https://www.vibe.com/features/ editorial/swizz-beatz-jay-z-alicia-keys-beyonce-global-citizen-festival-238228.

218 "Thank You, Lana," Jewish Voice for Peace, accessed December 15, 2021, https://secure. everyaction.com/ZZpV3y6jZEy55WkfkjftmA2?ms=PACBI.

219 David Brinn, "Livin' on More Than a Prayer," *The Jerusalem Post*, July 22, 2019, https://www. jpost.com/israel-news/culture/livin-on-more-than-a-prayer-596119.

220 J. K. Rowling, Simon Schama, et al., "Israel Needs Cultural Bridges, Not Boycotts," *The Guardian*, October 22, 2015, https://www.theguardian.com/world/2015/oct/22/israel-needs-cultural-bridges-not-boycotts-letter-from-jk-rowling-simon-schama-and-others.

221 David Sedley, "JK Rowling Tells Victims of Anti-Semitism 'You Aren't Alone,'" *The Times of Israel*, April 19, 2018, https://www.timesofisrael.com/ jk-rowling-tells-victims-of-anti-semitism-you-arent-alone.

222 Other signatories included William Morris Endeavor agent David Levy; notable art historian Simon Schama; English broadcaster, author, and parliamentarian Melvyn Bragg; Cohen Media Group former president Daniel Battsek; documentary film producer John Battsek; producer John Heyman; English writer Dame Hilary Mantel; and former entertainment attorney and founder of the Edge Group David Glick.

223 Tony Greenstein, "JK Rowling Responds to Palestinian Fan—Mia Oudeh," Tony Greenstein's Blog, October 31, 2015, https://azvsas.blogspot.com/2015/10/jk-rowling-responds-to-palestinian-fan.html.

224 "JK Rowling Speaks Out over Israel-Palestine Issue," Business Standard, October 28, 2015, https://www.business-standard.com/article/pti-stories/j-k-rowling-speaks-out-over-israel-palestine-issue-115102801494_1.html.

225 James Meadway, "Gil Scott Heron Cancels Israel Gig," Aletho News, April 25, 2010, https://alethonews.com/2010/04/26/gil-scott-heron-cancels-israel-gig.

226 "More Than 190 Hollywood Notables Sign Pro-Israel Statement Criticizing Hamas," Hollywood Reporter, August 23, 2014, https://www.hollywoodreporter.com/news/general-news/more-190-hollywood-notables-sign-727221.

227 Neil Young, Tell Me Why You Would Play for Apartheid Israel, "We appreciate Neil Young Archives for refraining from entertaining apartheid Israel," Facebook, June 20, 2019, https://www.facebook.com/Neil.Young.WhyPlay.Apartheid.Israel/posts/2356226454470531.

228 Jessica Steinberg, "Celine Dion Reschedules Tel Aviv Concerts for June 2021," The Times of Israel, June 10, 2020, https://www.timesofisrael.com/celine-dion-reschedules-tel-aviv-concerts-for-june-2021.

229 Janelle Griffith, "Manchester Arena Bomber's Brother Guilty of Killing 22 at Ariana Grande Concert," NBC News, March 17, 2020, https://www.nbcnews.com/news/world/manchester-arena-bomber-s-brother-guilty-killing-22-ariana-grande-n1161706.

230 "Tunisian Who Sang Duet with Israeli Gets Death Threats, Said Fired from His Job," The Times of Israel, December 27, 2020, https://www.timesofisrael.com/tunisian-who-sang-duet-with-israeli-faces-backlash-death-threats/?fbclid=IwAR1BLm6qEaDn_IwYNOOtL_3n20kvioY6BBoXRxgJ2nvLOV2NCgt6caTKT1s.

231 Lana Melman, "Women for Israel Sapphire Society Reception with Sarah Idan and Lana Melman," YouTube, uploaded November 13, 2020, https://www.youtube.com/watch?v=vWG_i5KoGGQ.

232 Nick Mason and Roger Waters, "Pink Floyd's Roger Waters and Nick Mason: Why Rolling Stones Shouldn't Play in Israel," Salon, May 1, 2014, https://www.salon.com/2014/05/01/pink_floyds_roger_waters_and_nick_mason_why_rolling_stones_shouldnt_play_in_israel.

233 Ethan Sacks, "Roger Waters Calls for Rolling Stones to Bail Out of Concert in Israel over Palestinian Question," *New York Daily News*, May 1, 2014, https://www.nydailynews.com/entertainment/music-arts/roger-waters-rolling-stones-boycott-israel-article-1.1775991.

234 William Booth and Ruth Eglash, "Pink Floyd Hit Out at Rolling Stones for Playing in Israel," *Sydney Morning Herald*, June 5, 2014, https://www.smh.com.au/world/pink-floyd-hits-out-at-rolling-stones-for-playing-in-israel-20140605-zrxzr.html.

235 Scott Whitlock, "One-Sided CBS Promotes Pink Floyd's Tirade Against 'Racist Regime' of Israel," *NewsBusters.org*, June 5, 2014, https://www.newsbusters.org/blogs/nb/scott-whitlock/2014/06/05/one-sided-cbs-promotes-pink-floyds-tirade-against-racist-regime.

236 "Sour Note: Rolling Stones Perform in Israel, to the Chagrin of Pink Floyd," *CBS News*, June 5, 2014, https://www.cbsnews.com/news/rolling-stones-perform-in-israel-despite-pink-floyds-boycott.

237 Annie Robbins, "Video: 'CBS This Morning' Runs Hard Hitting Spot on Boycott of Israel," *Mondoweiss*, June 5, 2014, https://mondoweiss.net/2014/06/morning-hitting-boycott.

238 Eliza Wilson and Shyam Dodge, "Rolling Stones Stars Mick Jagger, Ronnie Wood, and Charlie Watts Visit Jerusalem's Western Wall Before First Ever Israel Concert," *Daily Mail*, last modified June 6, 2014, https://www.dailymail.co.uk/tvshowbiz/article-2650048/Rolling-Stones-stars-Mick-Jagger-Ronnie-Wood-Charlie-Watts-visit-Jerusalems-Western-Wall-Israel-concert.html.

239 Eliza Wilson and Shyam Dodge, "Rolling Stones Stars Mick Jagger, Ronnie Wood and Charlie Watts Visit Jerusalem's Western Wall Before First Ever Israel Concert," *Daily Mail*, last modified June 6, 2014, https://www.dailymail.co.uk/tvshowbiz/article-2650048/Rolling-Stones-stars-Mick-Jagger-Ronnie-Wood-Charlie-Watts-visit-Jerusalems-Western-Wall-Israel-concert.html.

240 William Booth and Ruth Eglash, "Rolling Stones to Perform in Israel Despite Pressure from Pink Floyd Members to Cancel," *Washington Post*, June 4, 2014, https://www.washingtonpost.com/world/middle_east/rolling-stones-to-perform-in-israel-despite-pressure-from-pink-floyd-members-to-cancel/2014/06/04/29f2df78-eb42-11e3-b10e-5090cf3b5958_story.html.

241 Ethan Sacks, "Roger Waters Calls for Rolling Stones to Bail Out of Concert in Israel over Palestinian Question," *New York Daily News*, May 1, 2014, https://www.nydailynews.com/entertainment/music-arts/roger-waters-rolling-stones-boycott-israel-article-1.1775991.

242 Roger Cohen, "Let It Bleed," *New York Times*, June 9, 2014, https://www.nytimes.com/2014/06/10/opinion/cohen-let-it-bleed.html.

243 Jon Blistein, "Roger Waters Calls for Boycott of Israel," *Rolling Stone*, March 20, 2013, https://www.rollingstone.com/music/music-news/roger-waters-calls-for-boycott-of-israel-65804.

244 "Roger Waters in His Own Words," Anti-Defamation League, accessed December 15, 2021, https://www.adl.org/resources/fact-sheets/roger-waters-in-his-own-words.

245 Brittany Spanos, "Demi Lovato Apologizes for Accepting Controversial Trip to Israel," *Rolling Stone*, October 4, 2019, https://www.rollingstone.com/music/music-news/demi-lovato-israel-sponcon-apology-895137.

246 Anastasia Tsioulcas, "Palestinian Artists Call for Eurovision Boycott; Israel Responds with PR Campaign," NPR, May 10, 2019, https://www.npr.org/2019/05/10/722106820/palestinian-artists-call-for-eurovision-boycott-israel-responds-with-pr-campaign.

247 Ilana Kaplan, "Watch Madonna and Quavo Perform 'Future' in Controversial Eurovision Set," *Rolling Stone*, May 19, 2019, https://www.rollingstone.com/music/music-news/madonna-quavo-future-eurovision-controversy-837263.

248 Ilana Kaplan, "Watch Madonna and Quavo Perform 'Future' in Controversial Eurovision Set," *Rolling Stone*, May 19, 2019, https://www.rollingstone.com/music/music-news/madonna-quavo-future-eurovision-controversy-837263.

249 Matthew Strauss, "Radiohead Israel Performance Protested by Thurston Moore, Roger Waters, Desmond Tutu, More," *Pitchfork*, April 24, 2017, https://pitchfork.com/news/71475-radiohead-israel-performance-protested-by-thurston-moore-roger-waters-desmond-tutu-more.

250 Matthew Strauss, "Radiohead Israel Performance Protested by Thurston Moore, Roger Waters, Desmond Tutu, More," *Pitchfork*, April 24, 2017, https://pitchfork.com/news/71475-radiohead-israel-performance-protested-by-thurston-moore-roger-waters-desmond-tutu-more.

251 Ami Friedman, "Jay Leno: 'Hope not to go back to TV,'" *YNet.co.il*, May 14, 2021, https://www.ynet.co.il/articles/0,7340,L-4522291,00.html.

252 Amy Mitchell, Mark Jurkowitz, J. Baxter Oliphant, and Elisa Shearer, "Americans Who Mainly Get Their News on Social Media Are Less Engaged, Less Knowledgeable," Pew Research Center, July 30, 2020, https://www.journalism.org/2020/07/30/americans-who-mainly-get-their-news-on-social-media-are-less-engaged-less-knowledgeable.

253 Amy Mitchell, Mark Jurkowitz, J. Baxter Oliphant, and Elisa Shearer, "Americans Who Mainly Get Their News on Social Media Are Less Engaged, Less Knowledgeable," Pew Research Center, July 30, 2020, https://www.journalism.org/2020/07/30/americans-who-mainly-get-their-news-on-social-media-are-less-engaged-less-knowledgeable.

254 Amy Mitchell, Mark Jurkowitz, J. Baxter Oliphant, and Elisa Shearer, "Americans Who Mainly Get Their News on Social Media Are Less Engaged, Less Knowledgeable," Pew Research Center, July 30, 2020, https://www.journalism.org/2020/07/30/americans-who-mainly-get-their-news-on-social-media-are-less-engaged-less-knowledgeable.

255 "List of most-followed Facebook Pages," Wikipedia, last modified January 20, 2022, https://en.wikipedia.org/wiki/List_of_most-followed_Facebook_pages.

256 Katy Perry (@@katyperry), "I am! My prayers are for you guys tonight, SHALOM!!!" Twitter, August 22, 2011, https://twitter.com/katyperry/status/105579422312173569?lang=en.

257 Michelle Malkin, "What Happened When Katy Perry Tweeted 'Pray for Israel,'" UNZ. com, August 23, 2011, https://www.unz.com/author/michelle-malkin//2011/08/23/what-happened-when-katy-perry-tweeted-pray-for-israel.

258 Katy Perry (@@katyperry), "a kid asked me to pray for him & I did. I don't support ANY side of violence in ANY place for ANY reason," Twitter, August 23, 2011, https://twitter.com/katyperry/status/105885288131330048.

259 Demi Lovato (@@ddlovato), "I am an American singer. I was raised Christian and have Jewish ancestors." Instagram post, October 1, 2019, https://www.pinterest.se/pin/722053752741734834/.

260 Sam Prance, "Zara Larsson Calls Out Demi Lovato for Not 'Choosing Sides' in her Israel Apology," PopBuzz.com, October 4, 2019, https://www.popbuzz.com/music/artists/demi-lovato/news/israel-palestine-apology-zara-larsson.

261 "Accountability? I Don't Know Her: Demi Lovato Apologizes before Guilt-Tripping Fans over Her Controversial Israel Posts," Bossip, October 3, 2019, https://bossip.com/1795256/accountability-i-dont-know-her-demi-lovato-apologizes-before-guilt-tripping-fans-over-her-controversial-israel-posts/.

262 Scott Stump, "Demi Lovato Apologizes after Backlash over Free Trip to Israel," Today, October 3, 2019, https://www.today.com/popculture/demi-lovato-apologizes-after-backlash-over-free-trip-israel-t163862.

263 Alex Rodriguez (@@AROD), "Jerusalem, you are unforgettable. What a perfect finale to our first trip to this beautiful land," Twitter, August 2, 2019, https://twitter.com/arod/status/1157328532344848384.

264 Maariv Online, "Under BDS Pressure: Only 2,000 Show Up for Jennifer Lopez's Concert in Egypt," JPost, August 11, 2019, https://www.jpost.com/bds-threat/under-bds-pressure-only-2000-show-up-jenifer-lopezs-concert-in-egypt-598319.

265 Ashley Iasimone, "Lana Del Rey Says Her Decision to Perform in Israel Is 'Not a Political Statement,'" Billboard, August 19, 2018, https://www.billboard.com/music/pop/lana-del-rey-israel-concert-meteor-festival-statement-8470935.

266 Hella Kiefer, "Lana Del Rey Will Now Visit Palestine After Israel Concert: 'I Want Peace for Both.'" Vulture, August 21, 2018, https://www.vulture.com/2018/08/lana-del-rey-defends-plans-to-perform-in-israel.html.

267 Gab Ginsberg, "Lana Del Rey Postpones Israel Concert," *Billboard*, August 31, 2018, https://www.billboard.com/music/pop/lana-del-rey-postpones-israel-concert-tweet-8473151.

268 Gab Ginsberg, "Lana Del Rey Postpones Israel Concert," *Billboard*, August 31, 2018, https://www.billboard.com/music/pop/lana-del-rey-postpones-israel-concert-tweet-8473151.

269 Ashley Iasimone, "Lana Del Rey Says Her Decision to Perform in Israel Is 'Not a Political Statement,'" *Billboard*, August 19, 2018, https://www.billboard.com/music/pop/lana-del-rey-israel-concert-meteor-festival-statement-8470935.

270 Michelle Kim, "Lana Del Rey Says Performing in Israel 'Is Not a Political Statement,'" *Pitchfork*, August 19, 2018, https://pitchfork.com/news/lana-del-rey-says-performing-in-israel-is-not-a-political-statement.

271 Denise Petski, "Lana Del Rey Cancels Israel Concert a Week Before Performance after Backlash," *Deadline*, August 31, 2018, https://deadline.com/2018/08/lana-del-rey-cancels-israel-concert-after-backlash-israel-meteor-festival-palestine-1202455456.

272 David Horovitz, "Bruce Springsteen: I Really Need to Play in Israel," *The Times of Israel*, October 6, 2016, https://www.timesofisrael.com/bruce-springsteen-i-really-need-to-play-in-israel.

273 David Lange, "Billie Eilish Saying 'Hi Israel' Causes Haters to Say 'Bye Felicia,'" *IsraellyCool*, August 1, 2021, https://www.israellycool.com/2021/08/01/billie-eilish-saying-hi-israel-causes-haters-to-say-bye-felicia.

274 David Hellerman, "BDS Bullies Attack Pop Star Billie Eilish on Social Media," *World Israel News*, August 2, 2021, https://worldisraelnews.com/bds-bullies-attack-pop-star-billie-eilish-on-social-media.

275 "Neil Young's Upcoming Tel-Aviv, Israel Concert: 'Don't Feel Like Satan But I Am To Them,'" New Young News, July 4, 2014, http://neilyoungnews.thrasherswheat.org/2014/07/neil-youngs-upcoming-tel-aviv-israel.html.

276 Francesca Grecto, "Michael Jackson—Live in Israel (Dangerous Tour 1993)", YouTube, accessed January 27, 2022. https://www.youtube.com/watch?v=5Cs5r1fMHWQ.

277 David Brinn, "An Easy PiL to Swallow," *The Jerusalem Post*, updated August 3, 2017, https://www.jpost.com/arts-and-culture/music/an-easy-pil-to-swallow.

278 Brandon Gaille, "25 Good Hip Hop Demographics," BrandonGaille.com, February 5, 2015, https://brandongaille.com/25-good-hip-hop-demographics.

279 Nick Kimberley, "Jerusalem Quartet, Classical Music Review: Pleasure and Protest," *Evening Standard*, November 23, 2015, https://www.standard.co.uk/culture/music/jerusalem-quartet-classical-music-review-pleasure-and-protest-a3120866.html.

280 Yvette Deane, "BDS Activists Musically Protest Batsheva Dance Company," *The Jerusalem Post*, last modified July 11, 2018, https://www.jpost.com/Diaspora/ BDS-activists-musically-protest-Batsheva-Dance-Company-562240.

281 Stephi Wild, "50 NYers Protest Batsheva Dance Company for Whitewashing Israel's Repression," *Broadwayworld.com*, July 11, 2018, https://www.broadwayworld.com/ bwwdance/article/50-NYers-Protest-Batsheva-Dance-Company-For-Whitewashing-Israels-Repression-20180711.

282 Lana Melman, "BDS Plays a Nazi Tune outside Carnegie Hall," *The Algemeiner*, February 7, 2019, https://www.algemeiner.com/2019/02/07/bds-plays-a-nazi-tune-at-carnegie-hall.

283 "Protests Disrupt Proms Concert by Israel Philharmonic," BBC, September 2, 2011, https:// www.bbc.com/news/uk-14756736.

284 Aaron Bandler, "Israeli Orchestra Performs in Morocco Despite BDS Pressure," *Jewish Journal*, December 18, 2019, https://jewishjournal.com/news/israel/308672/ israeli-orchestra-performs-in-morocco-despite-bds-pressure.

285 Zach Pontz, "South African BDSers Sing 'Shoot the Jew' at Event Featuring Israeli Saxophonist," *The Algemeiner*, August 29, 2013, https://www.algemeiner.com/2013/08/29/ south-african-bdsers-sing-shoot-the-jew-at-event-featuring-israeli-saxophonist.

286 Sam Sokol, "South Africa BDS Leader Defends Call to 'Kill the Jew,'" *The Jerusalem Post*, September 2, 2013, https://www.jpost.com/jewish-world/jewish-features/ south-africa-bds-leaders-defends-call-to-kill-the-jew-325075.

287 Sam Sokol, "South Africa BDS Leader Defends Call to 'Kill the Jew,'" *The Jerusalem Post*, September 2, 2013, https://www.jpost.com/jewish-world/jewish-features/ south-africa-bds-leaders-defends-call-to-kill-the-jew-325075.

288 Itamar Eichner, "Norwegian Festival Boycotts Israeli Artists, Cites 'Occupation,'" *Ynet*, March 19, 2018, https://www.ynetnews.com/articles/0,7340,L-5181105,00.html.

289 Itamar Eichner, "Norwegian Festival Boycotts Israeli Artists, Cites 'Occupation,'" *Ynet*, March 19, 2018, https://www.ynetnews.com/articles/0,7340,L-5181105,00.html.

290 "Anti-Semitism in the Fashion World: Model Shunned Because She's Israeli," United with Israel, January 15, 2020, https://unitedwithisrael.org/ anti-semitism-in-the-fashion-world-model-shunned-because-shes-israeli.

291 Nick Hallett, "Edinburgh Fringe Bans Israeli Show," Breitbart, August 1, 2014, https://www. breitbart.com/europe/2014/08/01/edinburgh-fringe-bans-israeli-show.

292 Peter Beaumont, "Brian Eno Refuses to Let Israeli Dance Company Use His Music," Arab America, September 9, 2016, https://www.arabamerica.com/ brian-eno-refuses-to-let-israeli-dance-company-use-his-music.

293 David Grossman, *To the End of the Land* (New York: Vintage Books, 2008).

294 "Paradise Now," Wikipedia, last modified October 14, 2021, https://en.wikipedia.org/wiki/Paradise_Now.

295 Jenni Frazer, "Ahead of Summer Fests, Scotland's New Pro-Israel Network Stands Guard," *The Times of Israel*, August 5, 2015, https://www.timesofisrael.com/ahead-of-summer-fests-scotlands-new-pro-israel-network-stands-guard.

296 John Anderson, "Festival in Oslo Rejects Film by Roy Zafrani Citing Cultural Boycott of Israel," *New York Times*, August 19, 2015, https://www.nytimes.com/2015/08/19/movies/festival-in-oslo-rejects-film-by-roy-zafrani-citing-cultural-boycott-of-israel.html.

297 International Committee of the Red Cross in Israel and the Occupied Territories (@@ICRC_ilot), "Like many of you, this year we've also watched @@FaudaOfficial and noted a number of violations of #IHL," Twitter, December 27, 2020, https://twitter.com/ICRC_ilot/status/1343191291052634117.

298 International Committee of the Red Cross in Israel and the Occupied Territories (@@ICRC_ilot), "Hiking in the forest is good for you. Taking hostages is illegal in any circumstances," Twitter, December 27, 2020, https://twitter.com/ICRC_ilot/status/1343191291052634117.

299 International Committee of the Red Cross in Israel and the Occupied Territories (@@ICRC_ilot), "Like many of you, this year we've also watched @@FaudaOfficial and noted a number of violations of #IHL," Twitter, December 27, 2020, https://twitter.com/ICRC_ilot/status/1343191291052634117.

300 Lana Melman, "Liberate Art brings Ziggy Marley to Jewish National Fund event," YouTube, June 11, 2016, https://www.youtube.com/watch?v=m25LTlPRmcA&t=12s. See also Shiryn Ghermezian, "Ziggy Marley Raffirms Love of Israel in 'Shalom Award' Acceptance Speech (VIDEO)," *The Algemeiner*, November 25, 2015, https://www.algemeiner.com/2015/11/25/ziggy-marley-reaffirms-love-of-israel-in-shalom-award-acceptance-speech-video.

301 Michael Douglas, "Op-Ed: Michael Douglas Finds Judaism and Faces Anti-Semitism," *Los Angeles Times*, March 14, 2015, https://www.latimes.com/opinion/op-ed/la-oe-0315-douglas-anti-semitism-20150315-story.html.

302 Viva Sarah Press, "When Jay Leno Met Benjamin Netanyahu," ISRAEL21c, May 22, 2014, https://www.israel21c.org/when-jay-leno-met-benjamin-netanyahu.

303 Josef Federman, "Jay Leno Makes Comeback in Israel for Award Show," *Associated Press*, Post and Courier, last modified November 2, 2016, https://www.postandcourier.com/features/jay-leno-makes-comeback-in-israel-for-award-show/article_865bd7dd-f87f-5500-b70d-46d8bc4fd91a.html.

304 Josef Federman, "Leno to Host Award Ceremony in Israel," *Associated Press News*, May 9, 2014, https://apnews.com/article/d1a09312678b48678f44159f40916e00.

305 Associated Press, "Helen Mirren Discourages Israel Boycott," *Hollywood Reporter*, June 22, 2016, https://www.hollywoodreporter.com/news/general-news/helen-mirren-discourages-israel-boycott-905436.

306 Associated Press, "Helen Mirren Discourages Israel Boycott," *Hollywood Reporter*, June 22, 2016, https://www.hollywoodreporter.com/news/general-news/helen-mirren-discourages-israel-boycott-905436.

307 Wilshire Boulevard Temple, "Defending Artistic Expression," YouTube, October 31, 2017, https://www.youtube.com/watch?v=S6KU9wRSYR8.

308 Mark Pellegrino (@@MarkRPellegrino), "@@NessinhaG @@_MercuryV @@_nathy the alternatives for the Israelis are to fight or be destroyed. This is a choice FORCED upon them by the terrorists," Twitter, July 12, 2014, https://twitter.com/markrpellegrino/status/488045448356052992.

309 JTA, "Mayim Bialik 'Happy to Take a Public Bullet' over Israel Support," *The Times of Israel*, March 21, 2018, https://www.timesofisrael.com/mayim-bialik-happy-to-take-a-public-bullet-over-israel-support.

310 JTA, "Mayim Bialik 'Happy to Take a Public Bullet' over Israel Support," *The Times of Israel*, March 21, 2018, https://www.timesofisrael.com/mayim-bialik-happy-to-take-a-public-bullet-over-israel-support.

311 Lana Melman, "Bill Maher Asks 'Is BDS the Right Thing To Do?" *The Times of Israel*, August 21, 2019, https://blogs.timesofisrael.com/bill-maher-asks-is-bds-the-right-thing-to-do.

312 Ian Schwartz, "Bill Maher on Gaza Conflict: 'It's a War that Hamas Started'; 'People Die in Wars,'" *RealClearPolitics.com*, August 2, 2014, https://www.realclearpolitics.com/video/2014/08/02/bill_maher_on_israel-gaza_conflict_its_a_war_that_hamas_started_people_die_in_wars.html.

313 Paul Miller, "Hollywood Comes Together to Support Israel and Condemn Hamas," *The Algemeiner*, August 26, 2014, https://www.algemeiner.com/2014/08/26/hollywood-comes-together-to-support-israel-and-condemn-hamas.

314 "More Than 190 Hollywood Notables Sign Pro-Israel Statement Criticizing Hamas," *Hollywood Reporter*, August 23, 2014, https://www.hollywoodreporter.com/news/general-news/more-190-hollywood-notables-sign-727221.

315 In Hollywood, agents, managers, and executives often change affiliations and jobs. The listings here are only accurate as of the time of writing.

316 Debra Messing (@@DebraMessing), "2) The jews have lived in Israel for 4000 years. They are indigenous peoples," Twitter, May 20, 2021, https://twitter.com/debramessing/status/1395446976263725060.

317 Nicki Gostin, "Steven Van Zandt Calls Twitter Follower an 'Ignorant Obnoxious Idiot,'" *New York Daily News*, May 5, 2016, https://www.nydailynews.com/entertainment/gossip/steven-van-zandt-twitter-war-israel-boycott-article-1.2626147.

318 David Mamet, *The Wicked Son: Anti-Semitism, Self-Hatred, and the Jews (Jewish Encounters)* (New York: Knopf Doubleday Publishing Group, 2006), 100.